HIDDEN TREASURES: SEARCHING FOR GOD IN MODERN CULTURE

By James M. Wall

The Christian Century Press, Chicago, Illinois

ACKNOWLEDGMENTS

The author is responsible for these essays, but he cannot by any means take full credit for the finished product. Each piece herein received careful editing by David Heim, managing editor of the *Christian Century* magazine. Fact checking, proofreading and, in final book form, continuity clarification were carried out by Dean Peerman, senior editor of the *Century*. The cover design, typesetting and internal organization were handled by Miriam Loria, production associate for the *Century*. Lisa Tiede, *Century* subscription manager, was the overall production coordinator for the book. These essays originally appeared in the *Christian Century* between the years 1991 and 1997.

CONTENTS

QUESTIONS OF RIGHT AND WRONG

HOPES AND FEARS

FOREWORD

On the staff's card congratulating James M. Wall on his 25th year as editor of the *Christian Century*, I wrote "Happy *Silver* Anniversary; congratulations on keeping us in the *black*." That line referred to the fact that the magazine has outlasted many opinion journals and hundreds of other magazines through some hard times for print journalism. We have survived. To survive is not the most noble of achievements, but as a friend says, "If we don't survive, we don't do anything else, either."

Having shared a corridor where our pathways collide, we have had hundreds of occasions to discuss policy for the magazine he has so capably produced as well as to construct policy for the world around us, which we would like to change more than it wants to be changed. One key theme in Wall's editorial credo is this: predictable, ideological, party-line journalism is deadly. There must be surprise; there have to be occasions for grace—a theme that Joseph Sittler, one of Wall's mentors, would appreciate. Jim Wall is universally described as a political, social, cultural, theological and editorial liberal. Which he is. But liberalism has changed through his quarter century of editing, and Wall is alert to its changes just as he makes efforts to keep a religious voice in the center of the redefinitions.

Because there are surprises and graces and because there is little ideology on these pages, those who have predictable and stereotypical visions of liberalism in mind may be confused or disappointed. The editor has a number of (relatively) nice things to say not only about conservatives but about figures further to the right. He admires conviction, courage and the energy to speak up; if secular America or religious liberals will not find the voice, let other leaders jar mainstream believers and citizens out of their complacency.

There are tinges and twinges of nostalgia in these writings. You can take this editor out of his native Georgia, but you cannot take the Georgia out of this editor. (You can't take Wall out of Methodism or Methodism out of Wall, though I'm not sure all his Wesleyan fellow travelers will always discern or welcome the voice of Wesley whispering through his writings.)

In Wall's frequent critiques of the media, the academy and other often spiritually opaque elites, he sometimes suggests that there was a time not too long ago when speaking up for God and faith, for soul and spirit, was easier than it is now. The historian in me wants to do my own speaking up: I think that it is easier to get a hearing for things of the spirit in the public media or the secular university of 1997 than it was in, say, 1937, 1957 or 1977. What I like about Wall's critique of the religiously barren public sphere is that he does not always and only blame the ever-handy secularist bogey. He is also ready to blame religious voices for having too little to say.

Having more to say leads Wall to draw on a whole range of sources. He may reflect on a current film one week and expound a new book of philosophy the next. He regularly reports on conversations with fellow commuters or airplane seatmates. These reports get refracted through a sensibility formed by wide reading in theology, philosophy and political science and by engagements as citizen and churchperson.

Wall is too hopeful, restrained, gentle, ambiguous and ironic to thunder like Jeremiah. And there is nothing of Amos here. Of Amos it was said *"ihm fehlt die Liebe"*—he lacks love. Wall loves movies, politics, the church and books too much to drop Amos's plumb line in their spheres.

If these pieces are not jeremiads or amosiads, they may be hoseanads or isaianads. Hosea speaks for a Lord disappointed in love with a covenanted people. Isaiah I and II alike speak critically but with a hope for all the people. Wall lives in a world where God is active but often in disguise, and where signs of the spirit are waiting to erupt from novels, movie screens and bully pulpits. His hoseanads and isaianads help provide direction for fellow pilgrims in this mixed secular-religious culture and era.

Martin E. Marty

PREFACE

The editorials I write each week for the *Christian Century* are produced on deadline. The topics are often determined by the events of the week, and the articles are usually tied to a particular moment in history. Nevertheless, in a review of the writings of recent years a pattern does emerge. Many of the articles are an attempt to find God's grace at work in the world around us, to see how God's grace is trying to break through to us. In such discoveries or glimpses one has the sense of finding a hidden treasure. More often than not, God's presence is hidden. It is our task to be receptive to moments of grace that come to us in unexpected ways.

This collection is published in my 25th year as editor of the *Christian Century*. During that time my search for signs of God in modern culture has been conducted publicly on a regular basis. But the search has gone on longer than that.

Many years ago, during a bitterly cold Alaskan winter, I wrote a letter to Ed Danforth, the sports editor of the *Atlanta Journal*. Danforth had hired me as a sportswriter, but I had left the staff for what I presumed would be a brief interlude with the U.S. Air Force during the Korean War. I was on active duty at Elmendorf Air Force Base in Anchorage when I wrote to tell Danforth that I had decided to leave journalism and start studying to become a Methodist minister. Danforth's response was typical of him: "Wall, your trouble is that you have had one too many forced landings on the tundra."

He may have been right. Who among us can ever explain vocational choices, especially a career decision that audaciously claims to have been a call from One in charge of all landings everywhere. Maybe I was looking for God during that Air Force assignment and decided that some academic experiences might sustain me in any future forced landings.

I was aware at the time, I suppose, that a shift from what was truly a dream job, writing on sports for the newspaper I had read since I learned to read, was hard to make. But there was a call, as we Methodists describe it, that I felt I had to answer. Fortunately, a few years later I was able to combine editorial and theological interests.

I moved to the Chicago area for further graduate study in theology in 1959, thinking that I was headed for a career as a teacher. One day a professor took me aside. "Wall, you are a writer, stick to it. You will do more with what you have as a writer, and you will have a much better time than you would in a classroom." A few months later I began a run in religious journalism which has lasted for more than 35 years. During that time I have continued my search for God, realizing that my vocation is to conduct that search outside the structures of church and classroom. As this collection indicates, my exploration includes sports, films, fiction and politics.

My religious sensibility was formed early in life in the Deep South. Folk there are not necessarily more faithful in their religion than others, but they do seem to have a special receptivity to matters of the spirit. I'm not sure I understand why—though Flannery O'Connor and Walker Percy offer some insights.

My old boss Ed Danforth was in his own way a scholar of sports, and he conveyed his knowledge in metaphorical language. He was a pre-eminent writer about horse racing, and his annual report on the Kentucky Derby always served as a model of how to write under deadline about an event which in itself is not important but which can become important through the writing.

I also learned from Ralph McGill, who was editor of the *Atlanta Constitution* and wrote a daily column for the paper. This was in an era when it was very difficult for a white southerner to speak as he did of fairness and justice in race relations. McGill was also a superb sportswriter, the field in which he began his career. I recall being a copyboy assigned to sit in the press box with McGill at Georgia Tech's Grant Field and do whatever he needed me to do. He was writing a front-page feature on a football game between Tech and a school from Virginia.

For some reason, McGill did not arrive until half time. He sat down and asked me what had happened. I told him that Tech was ahead 6-0, and I told him the name of the player who had returned the opening kickoff more than 90 yards for the touchdown—which turned out to be the only score of the game.

On the basis of that bit of information, McGill wrote a lead for his story which evoked the memory of dead, departed Virginian heroes—the names of Lee and Jefferson were employed—who looked down with sadness at the path cut by a Georgia Tech player that led to the defeat of these Virginians on this particular field of battle on a sunny afternoon in Atlanta. It was beautiful writing, which did not so much tell what happened as evoke a tradition and a memory, albeit a distinctly southern memory. I determined to write somewhere close to the style and verve of Ralph McGill, a man who used language to convey a larger truth, connecting to a universe of the spirit as he described relatively mundane events. If any of the writing in this collection even begins to approach McGill's style and verve, I will be pleased.

James M. Wall
July 1997

SURPRISED BY THE SACRED

"In any case it is perfectly clear that the goal of all art—unless of course it is aimed at the 'consumer,' like a saleable commodity—is to explain . . . to people the reason for their appearance on this planet, or if not to explain, at least to pose the question."

Andrey Tarkovsky, Sculpting in Time

HOME, FAMILY, RELIGION

Everyone wants to know if 81-year-old Horton Foote is related to Shelby Foote, the gravel-voiced historian who graced Ken Burns's television series on the Civil War. So when I had the chance to visit with Foote I asked him about it. Yes, he answered, the two Footes are third cousins; their great-grandfathers were brothers. "And while we didn't grow up together, we have become friends; I was the voice of Jefferson Davis in that TV series," he added proudly.

The Foote cousins also share a writing talent. Horton has earned two Academy Awards for screenplays (for *Tender Mercies* and *To Kill a Mockingbird*), and in 1995 won a Pulitzer Prize for his play *The Young Man from Atlanta*. The production of that play brought him to Chicago, where it will run until its New York opening.

Like all his plays, *Young Man* is drawn from family stories. Foote's much-acclaimed *Orphans' Home Cycle* includes nine plays, the first of which begins in 1902 with the death of his real-life paternal grandfather and the remarriage of his grandmother. (Foote does not consider *The Young Man from Atlanta*, which features characters drawn from an aunt and uncle, as part of his *Orphans* cycle. "That series has ended; it was about my father's search for a home.")

Foote was raised as a Methodist in Wharton (population 3,000, "half white, half black"), where religion was so much a part of the culture that it wasn't at all unusual for a minister to greet a newcomer with the question, "Where were you baptized, Mr. Sledge?"—which is a scene in *Tender Mercies*. That 1983 film stars Robert Duvall as Mac Sledge, an alcoholic country singer whose life is turned around when he marries a young widow who sings in the Baptist choir. The movie offers a rarity in contemporary film: when Mac is baptized, along with his young stepson, the Baptist immersion is treated respectfully.

Foote, who left Texas at age 17 and who has lived in New York, New Hampshire and California, remains a a southern writer whose work is saturated with religion. When pressed on the topic, however, he worries that he might be accused of what he calls, nervously, "proselytizing." He need not worry; his writing does not proselytize, but it does reveal the integral, inescapable role religion plays in his characters' lives.

He delights in telling interviewers about how a young Texas boy who had never before seen a stage play launched a career as an actor, and then later became a writer of plays and of television and movie scripts: "When I was about nine or ten, there was this gray-haired, dignified man we would see walking along the sidewalk. My parents would tell me, in awed tones, after he passed us, that Mr. Armstrong had been working in the cotton fields of Mississippi, when he got a call to come to Texas to preach. And I really was fascinated by that call. My mother told me that he was a Baptist minister, but Methodists and Episcopalians could also get calls. My father, who wasn't very religious, told me that preachers didn't make much money. I think he was afraid I might get the call to preach.

"Then, when I was 11 years old, I got a call just as distinct as Mr. Armstrong's, but my call was to be an actor. And I never veered from that, until I began writing and only then did I stop acting."

The "call" that sent young Horton off to Broadway provides one of those nice ironies that so often occur in a Foote script. And there may also be a bit of irony in the fact that a boy raised in bedrock Protestantism left the Methodist Church and as an adult converted to Christian Science—a faith little known in the Texas of his childhood, but one he faithfully follows.

Asked by the *Christian Science Monitor* how his work deals with "the questions of goodness and 'the things which are not seen,'" Foote responded, "I'm rather wary of any stated thesis like that or of any sense of proselytizing. As an artist, as a writer, I don't consciously do that. I watch and I observe and I try to be as objective and truthful as I can to the human condition I see around me."

He succeeds in this assignment through his use of understated dialogue—exchanges described as "slow" by one Chicago critic. These polite conversations both cover and reveal deep pain and frustration, laced with longing and hope. A more positive assessment of Foote's style comes from *New York Post* critic Jerry Tallmer, who points to Foote's use of "dry irony which can sketch character in a line." For example, one of his noncycle plays, *Talking Pictures*, contains this exchange between Katie and Myra:

> Katie: "Willis says you're not going to Hell if you go to the picture shows."
> Myra: "I wasn't worried. Thank you anyway, Willis, for telling me."

The Protestant tradition (of Methodists, Baptists and "a few Episcopalians") which was such a force in Foote's childhood is always present in the background of his characters. Always, too, there is concern for why some people are able to cope with adversity and others cannot. Foote told one interviewer: "The earliest thing that I remember being puzzled by as a child was that kind of mystery. . . . I've never been able to explain it. . . . I think that there's something essential that you can't explain. . . . That's certainly what I'm trying to explore. And that remains a mystery to me."

Foote has said that his plays are about "dislocation, sibling rivalries, elopements, family estrangements, family reconciliations, and all the minutiae that make family life at once so interesting and yet at times so burdening." His writing is deceptively simple, filled with quiet exchanges between people who desperately want to understand what is happening to them but are constantly confronted by loss and suffering over which they have no final control.

Religion does not provide answers for Foote, but it does provide a context with which to struggle with mystery. His dialogue and narratives move his characters through sudden turns of fortune—the death of a parent or husband, the loss of a job—while in the background is southern Protestant culture, portrayed through the clichés of the community and the poetry of the gospel songs and romantic ballads he heard while sitting on the front porch in Wharton. Music is prominent in his plays, and it evokes the longing, sadness and hope of Foote's religious tradition.

Some Foote characters embrace religion, others resist it vigorously, but it is always there. Lily Dale Kidder, for example, in *The Young Man from Atlanta* turns to religion with considerable intensity after the death of her 37-year-old son, who drowns under mysterious circumstances. When I asked Foote about Lily Dale's faith, he said, "I don't know if I understand totally her religion; I tried to understand it. I do know that after the death of her son, it became a life force for her. She was always religious, but after his death, she became almost obsessional about it. This is very understandable. She gives up everything and begins a deep study of the Bible."

In *Young Man* Will Kidder loses his job at age 63, summarily fired by the son of the man with whom Kidder had started a produce supply company. The ever-present anxiety inherent in the economic insecurity of an adult who lived through the Depression is vividly portrayed. Will buys Lily Dale a house and new car in an effort to assuage her grief over the death of their son, but when he loses his job he is forced to turn to her for a loan. This is humiliating for a man whose entire life has been a quest for financial security and to provide for his family. It is painful to witness his disintegration as the play progresses, and it becomes apparent that Lily Dale may have been conned out of her money by the young man from Atlanta, who may or may not have been a close friend of their son.

I reminded Foote of the scene in *Tender Mercies* in which Mac Sledge, his life finally stable, married, with a young stepson he loves and a songwriting career back on track, loses his daughter in an automobile accident. Poking the ground of his garden, trying to get his emotions under control, Mac asks his wife, "Why did she have to die?" Then he adds, "I never trusted happiness; I never have, and I never will." Then Mac goes across the road and starts playing catch with his son—still living with his grief, but somehow moving forward.

About that scene, Foote commented, "We all have this great fear that if we are given something nice, it is going to be taken away." But Mac's despair, Foote said, "is only a momentary thing; if one deeply believed [in such despair] all the time one couldn't get out of bed in the morning. I think, on the contrary, there is this sense of mending, of healing [in the film]."

Foote has his own way of coping with what he calls "life's vicissitudes." Foote recently completed work on a screenplay for *Alone*, a movie produced for Showtime about a man whose wife has just died. Foote wrote the screenplay after "meditating" on the death of his own wife three years ago. The writer whom Public Television's Jim Lehrer describes as "a national treasure" continues to create stories of suffering and hope. Why does he do it? "I guess I finally, deeply inside myself, do feel that in spite of all the chaos around us, there's an awful lot to celebrate in human beings."

A SOULFUL AFTERNOON IN THE LIBRARY

I was browsing through the recent-arrivals shelf at the public library when one of our librarians stopped to tell me how much she liked a film she had just seen on video. A film critic always hates to admit that he hasn't seen a film, so I was relieved when the movie turned out to be *Cinema Paradiso*. Yes, I had seen it and yes, it was a fine work of art. It is much more than that, she said. "Anyone who doesn't like that picture doesn't have a soul."

A busy library is not the place to begin a discussion on the nature of the soul and how and whether one can lose one's soul. But as I resumed my browsing I pondered the matter and decided she was right. Viewers who find *Cinema Paradiso* just another subtitled yarn about village life in wartime Italy are dangerously close to functioning without a soul. If we define the soul as that dimension of our existence which is connected to the ultimate in the universe, then I am prepared to agree that one needs an active alert soul to resonate with a movie like *Cinema Paradiso*. This picture invites us to connect with the depths of reality, to mesh with the ultimate.

To engage in an intellectually responsible discussion on this topic in our time we must first define the soul, prove its existence and then explain how it can disappear. This battery of questions cows us into polite submission, for we have been educated to believe that truth must be measurable. We must assemble data according to scientific methods and offer a conclusion that will stand until someone else comes along with newer, more valid data. We are victims and practitioners of the modern mind-set that relies on what Italian philosopher Gianni Vattinio describes as "the reduction of everything to exchange-value" (*The End of Modernity*).

One way to counter this model of reality is to speak anecdotally—an approach scholars tend to find objectionable. How often we are told: "The evidence you are giving is purely anecdotal, a collection of random stories that can't stand up to the harsh demands for rational validation." What are the central questions that matter, according to this view? Not how should I live, but will it succeed? Will it work? What is the bottom line? The more data we accumulate to prove that something works, the more validity it possesses. Anecdotal evidence is not sufficient for serious conversation.

Consider, as just one example, the man whose eyesight was restored by Jesus. When questioned by his friends as to how such a miracle could have happened, the man replies, anecdotally, "All I know is that I once was blind, and now I can see." Nice, but not enough to verify the healer as a reliable practitioner.

French philosopher Jean-François Lyotard maintains that one of the deadening contributions of modernity is to limit knowledge to "quantities of information" that are "translatable into computer language." In a section on Lyotard in *An Introductory Guide to Post-Structuralism and Postmodernism*, Madan Sarup points out how Lyotard explicitly contrasts scientific language, the language of verification and falsification, with narrative or story, "which certifies itself without having recourse to argumentation and proof." Narratives are "fables, myths, legends," which scientists regard as part of a "different mentality: savage, primitive, underdeveloped."

This embrace of measured reality as the only valid reality is at the opposite end of the spectrum from an equally irresponsible dependence on emotion alone. We would not survive as an organized society if we all relied only on John Wesley's dictum: "If your heart is right, give me your hand." A more balanced approach is essential. (Wesley balanced it with stern disciplines of thought and action.) But the soul shrivels when it is not open to experiential connections with the ultimate. Our obsession with measured reality ill prepares us for God's strange, undeserved and unexpected gifts of grace.

Describing a period in his career when his health was bad and his spirits low, filmmaker Ingmar Bergman confessed to a friend, "I'm about to lose my joy. I can feel it physically. It's running out. I'm just drying up, inside." Bergman recalled how Johann Sebastian Bach discovered that his wife and two of their children had died while he was away on a trip. In his diary Bach wrote, "Dear Lord, may my joy not leave me." In his autobiography Bergman wrote: "All through my conscious life, I . . . lived with what Bach calls his joy. It . . . carried me through crisis and misery and functioned as faithfully as my heart, sometimes overwhelming and difficult to handle, but never antagonistic or destructive. Bach called this state his joy, a joy in God."

To lose one's joy is to lose one's soul. Our existence is too crowded with burdensome tasks and unexpected setbacks for us to assume that alone we can overcome what confronts us. Bach's experience of joy continues with us through his music. Bergman's constant struggle between the experience of grace and despair is permanently available in his films. Both Bach and Bergman testify that holding on to joy is no easy assignment. But without joy, the ability to connect with the ultimate, we are left with only the hollow certainty of measured reality.

FILMS WITH A BAD ATTITUDE

Michael and Diane Medved agreed when they got married that their home would not have a television set. It may seem strange for one of the nation's most visible film critics to live without television, especially since his own public television program, *Sneak Previews*, draws consistently high ratings. But after you spend some time with Michael Medved, as I did recently on one of his twice-monthly visits to Chicago to tape *Sneak Previews*, you soon discover that a keystone in his life is discipline. Keep the set out of the house and neither children nor adults are tempted to waste time on trivial viewing pursuits.

Sneak Previews began with Chicago newspaper critics Roger Ebert and Gene Siskel. When they shifted to commercial syndication, PBS tried several combinations and finally settled on the team of Medved and Jeffrey Lyons. Lyons, who also works as a critic for WNBC-TV in New York, has been the better known of the pair, but Medved's book *Hollywood vs. America: Popular Culture and the War on Traditional Values* (HarperCollins) has attracted wide comment, much of it venomous.

From the fury of the attacks on his book (already in its second printing), one would think he wants to establish a national censorship board run by Donald Wildmon and Pat Buchanan. Peter Biskind, for example, wrote in *Premiere*: "There would be no point in discussing a book as repellent and ill-argued as Michael Medved's were it not the fact that it is getting so much attention." But the attacks do not appear to have undermined Medved's upbeat approach, which contrasts nicely with Lyons's more worldly and at times cynical style.

The chemistry between Medved and Lyons explains some of the program's success. They both obviously share a love for film, as was evident in their fast-paced conversation on the ride to the airport. Lyons challenged me to name the actors who played in *Twelve Angry Men*. Henry Fonda and Lee J. Cobb are easy, he said; to qualify as a film buff you must know the others. Lyons was in a hurry to get back to New York. Medved was anxious to reach Los Angeles before the start of the Sabbath.

Medved is an observant Jew. He is also a student of the Torah and a firm believer in traditional religious values, values he is convinced the film industry hates and demeans. Medved laughs at the charge that he favors censorship, and a reading of his book reveals that the charge is unjust. Medved wants the First Amendment to prevail, but he thinks the film industry has an attitude problem—a deep hostility to traditional values.

In his attacks on the film industry Medved likes to disarm liberal critics with this three-part question: Was racism routine in the movies of the 1930s? (Yes.) *Was Gone with the Wind* an example of this racism? (Yes.) Is *Gone with the Wind* a bad movie? (No.) The issue, he insists, is not quality, but attitude. More than 50 years after *GWTW* presented a host of clichés about blacks, the industry still conveys images of bigotry and it consistently undermines values. Given the option of making "uplifting" films or degrading ones, the industry chooses degradation.

Medved has gained the industry's attention because, unlike most religious conservatives who attack movies, he is an insider. His recognition of the difference between artistic and exploitative films leads him to argue that a film like *Silence of the Lambs*, while "dazzling" and "artfully executed," with "brilliant and intense" acting, is a lurid freak show.

I told Medved that some of us have worked for years to convince religious people that movies, while commercial products, have enormous potential, as art, to probe reality and to be receptive to moments of grace. I told him that (as I have argued before) the garbage that exists in the film world is the price we pay for artistic freedom. Medved responded by saying he is primarily interested in addressing an industry that has exploited its freedom and become a "poison factory."

Medved has the zeal of a prophet, and he is driven by a strong religious faith. Though Orthodox in conviction, in deference to the secular environment in which he works he keeps his yarmulke in his coat pocket, available for special occasions. If he were to wear the yarmulke during his program, he remarked, "everything I say would be interpreted as an officially religious point of view."

According to Medved, five times as many Americans attend church as attend movies. Hence an an accurate rendering of American culture would acknowledge the importance of religion in people's lives. He calls attention to three "big-budget medical melodramas—*Dying Young* (with Julia Roberts), *The Doctor* (with William Hurt) and *Regarding Henry* (with Harrison Ford)"—that feature protagonists facing "dire illnesses and long hospitalizations, with life and death hanging dramatically in the balance." At no point in any of these films, he complains, is there a reference to prayer, to God, or even to the possibility that when people are faced with life-threatening illnesses, religion could be a source of support. What is behind this omission? Medved thinks it is the film industry's contempt for traditional values.

Furthermore, Medved contends, the industry's attitude is costly to itself, because people are staying away from the kind of films that Hollywood produces. Medved's critics have challenged his data on this point, citing the box-office success of some of the films he decries and arguing that the industry is primarily motivated by the need to sell tickets, not by its attitude toward traditional values. But Medved thinks the industry is willing to lose money in order to attack religion and the family, to glorify ugliness and to indulge in (to use some of his catchy chapter headings) "the urge to offend," "the infatuation with foul language," "the addiction to violence," "hostility to heroes" and "bashing America."

Two recent films seem to bolster his case. Whoopie Goldberg's light comedy, *Sister Act*, contains very little sex, violence or profanity, and it has made money. Goldberg plays a gangster's mistress who hides out as a nun after witnessing a murder. The movie has an upbeat ending when Goldberg's church choir sings Motown-style hymns for the pope. Goldberg, Medved says, wanted her character to use more profanity so as to have a harder "edge." The Disney studio refused, and as a result she, Disney and audiences gained a successful film that comes about as close to a general-audience picture as one is likely to find these days.

Hero, a film with Dustin Hoffman, was not so wise. Hoffman insisted on considerable profanity in order to "realize" his character. Medved thinks this undercut the picture's potential to be a modern-day Frank Capra film. "Dustin's insistence on 12 'f' and 's' words cost that picture $10 million at the box office."

Such counting of words and sex scenes appears to place Medved in the camp with Wildmon and a moralism that has no regard for aesthetic context. And the sweeping nature of some of his condemnations undermines his case. He doesn't even spare *The Little Mermaid*, for example, arguing that an otherwise charming children's animated film shows children as smarter than adults and undermines the teaching authority of the family. He is more on target with his condemnation of *Home Alone Two*, a film that is little more than a series of incidents of cruelty to dumb adults.

Medved is also open to the charge of Wildmonism in the way his attacks on films that deal with the afterlife make no distinction between the clearly exploitative films and the ones that are thoughtfully made. His keen sense of film aesthetics and history, evident on his television program, is brushed aside in his zealous attack on the industry.

Confronted with this charge, Medved insists that the overall context of a film does concern him. He praises *The Lover*, for example, which in depicting the teen-age romance of French author Marguerite Duras contains strong sexual content. "Yes, this is a graphic film, but it is never pornographic; it emphasizes tenderness." Such nuances are ignored by those who dismiss Medved as a prude.

Medved's crusade against Hollywood has fulfilled a prophecy a friend made when he confided his plans to write the book: "If you insist on going forward with something like this, you are going to become the most hated man in Hollywood." He doesn't mind the risk, he writes, "if the ensuing controversy will serve to open minds, and to encourage both producers and consumers of popular entertainment to examine its content with fresh eyes."

Since Hollywood is a profit-driven industry, short on forgiveness for those who interfere with that goal, Medved pays a price for his crusade. But he can't help himself. He is angry at the film industry for misusing an artistic and entertainment medium he loves. Catch him on *Sneak Previews*. He is the one with the mustache and the yarmulke tucked out of sight.

KIDS' STUFF

L ately I haven't had time to read the papers, as I have been building a mouseproof closet against a rain of mice. But sometimes, kindling a fire with last week's *Gazette*, I glance through the pages and catch up a little with the times." That's how E. B. White opened a short essay in *Harper's* magazine in October 1938. White predicted with chilling accuracy the way the proliferation of information via television can diminish our lives rather than enrich them. "I believe television is going to be the test of the modern world, and that in this new opportunity to see beyond the range of our vision we shall discover either a new and unbearable disturbance of the general peace or a saving radiance in the sky." A speaker at a recent Nashville conference on media and the family quoted that passage of White's (discovered, I later learned, on an Internet collection of quotations) and suggested that television was rapidly becoming a disturbance.

Television was very much in its infancy when White wrote his essay. He recalled having attended "a television demonstration at which it was shown beyond reasonable doubt that a person sitting in one room could observe the nonsense taking place in another." Nevertheless, the experience was striking enough ("By paying attention I could see the whites of a pretty woman's eyes") to convince

White that television was "tremendously important—more so than the ebb and flow of armies."

We have clearly failed the test that White described. We have allowed market forces to control television—and the rest of our modern communications media—to such a degree that the lowest common denominator of interest prevails. A free society rises or falls on the exercise of a collective responsibility. When we fail to respond to the needs and vulnerabilities of our citizens, we revert to the law of the jungle, permitting only the powerful to determine how we shall live.

Anger over the absence of responsibility surfaced at the Nashville conference, but the usual media industry voices were heard as well, pushing, as is their custom, individual rights over community responsibility. After attending the conference I decided that the obsession with individual rights—the right to make money or to write, say or do what I please—should be exposed for what it is: a form of fundamentalism that accepts one worldview as absolute and rejects all others as encroachments on the true faith.

My insight was reinforced when I saw *Kids*, a movie that follows a group of young teenagers through a day and night of sex, drugs and violence. *Kids* is director Larry Clark's first movie, but it is not his first venture into depicting the empty hedonism of young teenagers. In 1971 he published a book of photographs of young people in his hometown of Tulsa "shooting up, having sex, messing around, playing tough guys," as one writer describes it. His film continues that theme in a style of a photographer with a convincing script. The picture is unsparing in its depiction of a group of children without any interest other than getting enough sex and drugs to keep them out of touch with reality. (One particularly despairing sequence centers on four young boys who look to be around 11, sitting together on a sofa, smoking dope.)

Telly, a central character, prides himself on his ability to seduce virgins. Two of his conquests are shown at length, complete with a piteous plea from one girl who cries, "It hurts." Jennie, one of Telly's earlier victims, discovers that she is HIV positive. She wanders about the city, looking for Telly to tell him about her condition. At one party she takes pills that leave her barely awake. Stumbling into a bedroom, she finds Telly engaged in his latest conquest. She watches for a time and then falls onto a sofa. The film ends when a friend of Telly's finds her asleep and rapes her.

This is raw stuff when it involves adults, and is ugly and horrifying when it involves children. Which brings us back to the issue of responsibility. The rating board of the Motion Picture Association of America correctly gave the picture an NC-17 rating, the designation for pictures forbidden to anyone under 17. That rating has its economic cost to the filmmakers, since most theaters and major video chains refuse to handle NC-17 films.

Kids, made as an independent production, was first shown at the Sundance Film Festival, where it elicited some praise and some disgust. Miramax Films, a subsidiary of the Disney Company, obtained distribution rights to *Kids*, fully aware that it would probably be rated NC-17 and thus be unreleasable by Miramax since Disney will not distribute an NC-17 picture.

Harvey and Bob Weinstein, who run Miramax, entered *Kids* in the prestigious Cannes Film Festival and began an extensive campaign to convince critics that *Kids* is an important work of art that should be given the more profitable R rating, which allows parents to take their youngsters to the film and also opens up the video and cable television markets. (R-rated films on cable's various movie channels are easily available to children of any age who know how to program their VCRs, or whose parents don't care what they watch on cable.)

Critic Roger Ebert of the *Chicago Sun-Times*, a cohost of a popular television movie review program, emerged as a major supporter of *Kids* after interviewing director Larry Clark at Cannes. Before the film opened in Chicago, Ebert wrote that *Kids* is "a blunt warning for kids engaging in risky behavior, and a wake-up call for their parents . . . Watching *Kids* is fascinating, yet depressing. The movie has an unstudied authenticity that convinces you it knows exactly what it's talking about."

True, it is a well-made film. But what responsibility does the community have to prevent this graphic film from being available to children? Ebert quotes Clark: "It's not for all kids under 17, but it's for some kids under 17. I want people to see the movie. I want parents to go with their kids. But the kids have to be able to get in. Because this movie shows things that are a reality in this world." To which I must respond, "Get real, Larry." A rating doesn't distinguish between "some" and "all" kids. Ebert made no effort to challenge Clark's notion that "some" kids will see his movie with their understanding parents who will then take them down the street for a milk-shake and a heart-to-heart chat about AIDS.

Ebert and Clark seem to feel that *Kids* is a training film for kids—that it will discourage them from misconduct. I haven't heard that argument used for movies since the early days of pornography when hard-core pictures were preceded by a warning from a man wearing a doctor's smock about the terrible things viewers were about to witness.

Miramax made a final effort to move *Kids* out of the NC-17 category through a screening before the appeals board (made up of industry representatives and two religious advisers). High-priced defense attorney Alan Dershowitz was brought in to argue that children would benefit from seeing *Kids*, but the appeals board upheld the original rating.

In defiance of the system under which Miramax had sought the R rating, the Weinstein brothers refused to accept the NC-17 rating and released the film through a company they formed for the sole purpose of distributing *Kids*. The company is called Excalibur (to evoke King Arthur, a longtime Disney favorite?). Then, in a final bit of cynicism, ads for the film carry the line: "Warning: No one under 18 will be admitted without a parent or legal guardian." To the casual observer this may look like corporate concern for the young, especially with that ominous use of "warning," but it is in fact the same limitation (with a year's difference in age) the MPAA provides for the Restricted rating that the MPAA refused to give to Miramax.

In England the government runs the rating system, which has specific age levels as to suitability and is backed up by local police enforcement. The U.S. system of industry self-regulation is preferable to the English system, but a voluntary regulation system can survive only if its participants act in a responsible manner and abide by the rules they set for themselves.

THE PICTURES INSIDE OUR HEADS

Richard D. Heffner recently examined the explosive response to Oliver Stone's movie *JFK* and concluded that what really disturbs Stone's critics is that he represents a new and powerful kind of historian, one who is "fully determined to have his own way with the pictures inside our heads." Stone's "mind-boggling special effects, his rapid cuts and purposeful edits, his musical up-beats and down-beats, his endless flashbacks and flash-forwards, all play with our heads, mold our perceptions so much more effectively than the more linear media ever did."

What's interesting about *JFK*, Heffner quotes Stone as saying, is that "it's one of the fastest movies. . . . It's like splinters to the brain. We have 2,500 cuts in there, I would imagine. We had 2,000 camera setups. We're assaulting the senses . . . in a sort of new-wave technique. We admire MTV editing technique and we make no bones about using it. We want to . . . get to the subconscious . . . and certainly seduce the viewer into a new perception of . . . what occurred in Texas that day."

Heffner, himself a historian, finds *JFK* filled with "not-quite-provable speculations about the end of Camelot," but he is intrigued by the angry response to the film on the part of print media and television journalists. Heffner, who is also chairman of the motion picture industry's film rating system, suggests that the anger of the "lords of print" derives from their awareness that Stone and his "fellow celluloid/video Pied Pipers will become our nation's leading storytellers." The age of Gutenberg is experiencing its last gasp. We may dislike their vision, but these new storytellers "will set our national agenda, interpret our national future, just as the scribblers themselves had done until these last sputtering days of the 20th century."

The Gutenberg era has had an important connection with

Protestantism. Under the slogan "sola Scriptura," Protestants translated the Bible into the vernacular, and with the help of the press distributed Bibles to an unprecedented number of people. With Gutenberg's printing press the story of creation, fall and redemption was put into linear form, and Protestants have always been proud of their control over the biblical narrative of redemption. This was a notable advance, but also a major loss because it shifted the church's focus from visual images to the printed page. Critics' hostility toward Stone's imagistic form of history has a parallel in Protestants' hostility to visual art, and their corresponding insistence that print is superior to any other form of communication. Along with this preference goes a modern bias against artistic work, which is deemed irrelevant to the business of fact-gathering.

Heffner's remarks about the last gasp of the Gutenberg age relate directly to the mainline churches' dependence on print media to convey their message. The community that formalized the Bible expressed itself in signs and symbols. Its members pointed to a story with a beginning and an end, but this narrative is not limited by time or space. It is not just a linear narrative. It is a work of art, forged by a community of believers. It is a document that continually surprises and provokes. Its power lies not in the sequence of events it describes but in its power to transform our vision. It is a narrative that asks for commitment, not agreement.

The Bible is crammed with images that assault the senses, and their intention is certainly to "seduce the viewer into a new perception" of reality. That seductive process began in lonely encounters between God and Moses on a mountain, God and Daniel in the lions' den, and God and Jesus in a garden. A faithful community sanctified the stories of these encounters and declared them valid expressions of God's reality.

This notion of a transcendent source to the narrative is especially difficult to grasp in our era. We prefer to live by Protagoras's dictum that "man is the measure of all things." And in order for Protagoras's "man" to maintain this fiction of self-sufficiency, he tries to "measure" all things, especially through stories that move in a linear sequence.

But the Christian knows that stories are not bound by their linear shape, that the meaning of stories goes beyond the facts they portray. Art and faith converge in a protest against the elevation of linearity as the final word about reality. The Christian knows that the dichotomy between "truth" as a linear narrative and "truth" as shaped by images and the "pictures inside our heads" must be bridged—and that it is bridged in the faith that God creates and redeems reality and that God is the source of all that we are and will be.

Lutheran theologian Joseph Sittler respected the power of linear narrative, but he was constantly reminding us that to receive the full majesty of the biblical story we must accept it as an uncontrollable and unpredictable work of art. In one essay he pointed out how often the Gospels speak of unexpected "bestowals of grace," as in such phrases as "and suddenly . . . and on the way he met . . . now it happened that . . . there stood before him a man." It is "in the midst of the many-threaded, wild unsystematic of the actual," said Sittler, that "the not-expected was crossed and blessed by the not-possible."

REMEMBERING THE '50S

Pass it on. Dan Wakefield is one of us. His autobiography *Returning: A Spiritual Journey* gave it away, but secular critics, always nervous with anything that smacks of the "spiritual," prefer to think of Wakefield as either an evocative novelist with a special talent for describing the struggles of a midwestern kid who made it big in New York City and Hollywood or as a talented essayist who understands the ambiguities of modern culture. But Wakefield belongs in the same category as Bill Moyers, Garrison Keillor, Robert Coles, Garry Wills and novelists like Sue Miller, Reynolds Price and John Updike: they are authors who have gained an audience in the secular world without sacrificing their religious sensibilities.

Wakefield's best-known novel is *Starting Over*, a fictionalized autobiography which was made into a successful motion picture with Burt Reynolds playing Wakefield. His other novels, which include *Selling Out* and *Home Free*, feature candid but gentle portrayals of young men caught between the harsh restrictions of conscience and the joy/pain of sex. Wakefield writes of this conflict with an honesty that earned him some initial criticism in his native Indianapolis. In his fiction Wakefield captures with pathos and humor the dark side of his search for meaning. More recently, in *Returning*, Wakefield confessed that after a decades-long struggle against the bland piety of his youth, he found that he was unable to find peace until he gave up all the artificial props—alcohol, drugs, psychiatry, aimless sex—and returned to what he had been running away from: a connection with God.

In his *New York in the Fifties*, a loving remembrance of a circle of political and literary radicals in rebellion against the blandness of the Eisenhower era, Wakefield is still writing his spiritual autobiography, as he confided recently. He seems to believe that the way to spiritual growth is through personal honesty. Thus students who take his increasingly popular seminar on spiritual renewal begin by writing about their own embarrassing moments.

In his earlier work, Wakefield was the quintessential Protestant writer, determined to confront his own experiences. He was handicapped, he thought, by the fact that he could never escape that hound of heaven that traveled with him on an overnight train from Indianapolis to New York City's Grand Central Station back in 1952. In New York Wakefield absorbed the intellectual excitement of Columbia University by day and plunged into boozy collegiate discussions over numerous pitchers of beer by night. After graduation the nightly sessions continued in a Greenwich Village community that included James Baldwin, Joan Didion, John Gregory Dunne (Didion's future husband), Jack Kerouac, Murray Kempton, Nat Hentoff, Gay Talese, Norman Podhoretz and Norman Mailer. Wakefield celebrates this community in New York in the '50s, which began as an essay on Baldwin, at whose Village apartment Wakefield met jazz musicians, authors and intellectuals. He expanded the book to include interviews with other friends. When Wakefield returned to the Village to do research for the book, he went back to the White Horse Tavern, where Dylan Thomas had his last drink before he died at age 39 in nearby St. Vincent's Hospital.

"There's a plaque on the wall now indicating the table where the poet had his last drink, but in the old days it was one of an insider's privileges to know, and reveal the sacred spot to newcomers," Wakefield writes. Cut off from any traditional sense of the sacred, the White Horse regulars turned to psychiatry for their faith and the tavern for their church. The analyst "became our priest, garbed in his vestments of three-piece dark flannel suit, and his orthodoxy became our religion. Whether one partook of it or not, this communion on the couch was part of a dialogue and texture of our time and place," Wakefield recalls, but adds: "I lay down on the couch of Freudian psychoanalysis in the fifties and rose up six years later in anger and disillusionment."

In his spiritual quest Wakefield encountered several mentors, people who infiltrated his life and whose presence was still with him when he finally decided it was time to give up drinking and "return" to himself. Wakefield identifies Dorothy Day, Norman Eddy and Mark Van Doren as three of those mentors. "What drew me to [Day's] Catholic Worker movement, first as a journalist and then as a friend and sympathizer," he notes, was "a real mystique that called to young people of the fifties and drew them from all across the country, offering in the midst of the grim poverty of the Bowery something that all the glittering affluence around us lacked—a spirit, a purpose, a way of transcending self through service that those who came still vividly remember."

That same blend of spirituality and practicality was evident in Eddy, a minister "I was prepared not to like." Looking for stories to sell as a free-lancer, Wakefield had heard of the East Harlem Parish on East 100th Street, but he was uneasy about meeting the pastor, who he feared would be "some kind of long-faced missionary who'd warn me darkly of the wages of sin" and worse yet "would try to recruit me for Jesus." He found instead an "open, vital man with an easy laugh and a sense of the ridiculous as well as the divine, and I had to admire him in spite of my prejudice against preachers, especially Protestants, because he wasn't preaching his message so much as living it."

The practical commitment of Day and Eddy helped Wakefield bridge the gap between his negative feeling toward his Indiana piety and his longing for spiritual meaning. But it was Van Doren who restored to Wakefield a critical dimension in his spiritual search. In a college course on narrative art, Van Doren introduced his students (or reintroduced in Wakefield's case) to the New Testament. Wakefield recalls Van Doren's startling insistence that Jesus "was the most ruthless of men," ruthless in "following his conception of truth and iron in his will." In the context of the popular religion of the '50s, with its "feel good, be successful" motif, Van Doren's version of Jesus provided the intellectually hungry Wakefield with a spiritual leader he could respect.

Armed with this new understanding, Wakefield wrote "Slick Paper Christianity" for the *Nation*, a devastating attack on popular Protestantism as exemplified by the Methodist family magazine, *Together*. He described the now-defunct journal, which had a circulation of 1 million, as something of a Rotarian periodical for a Christian club. (*Together*, which happened to be edited by a former editor of the *Rotarian* magazine, annually selected an all-Methodist all-star football team.)

Van Doren was also a mentor for Columbia graduate Thomas Merton, who speaks appreciatively of Van Doren in his celebrated autobiography *The Seven Storey Mountain*. In describing his conversion to the Catholic Church, Merton writes of "how easily and sweetly it had all been done with all the external graces that had been arranged along my path by the kind providence of God." External graces also seem to have guided young Dan Wakefield on his path from Indianapolis to New York City, to Mark Van Doren's classroom, and to a remarkably creative community in New York in the '50s. Pass it on.

THE ENDLESS QUEST FOR THE PERFECT NOVEL

Summertime, and the living may not be easy, but it is a good time to embark once again on the quest to find the perfect novel. Granted, perfection is unattainable, but like the holy grail it must be sought, if for no other reason than that the quest itself is a goad, pushing the earnest reader to the library or the bookstore.

One summer a few years back the quest was sparked by a brief mention in *Variety* that the filmmaking team of Ismail Merchant and James Ivory had selected their next project. I had just seen their *Howards End*, based on the novel by E. M. Forster, a writer whose work Merchant and Ivory had earlier mined successfully with *A Room with a View* and, less successfully, *Maurice*. The team is at its best with late 19th- and early 20th-century British tales of manners and repressed sexuality, elegantly presented with scenes of green English countryside and properly managed houses. Their latest venture follows that pattern by taking up the work of contemporary author Kazuo Ishiguro.

Anthony Hopkins, who plays Henry Wilcox in *Howards End*, had been signed, *Variety* reported, for a film based on Ishiguro's 1989 novel *The Remains of the Day*. Not every proposed film makes it to the screen, but just the possibility of Hopkins being reunited with Merchant-Ivory sent me to the library to read Ishiguro. What I found was as close as I expect to get to the experience of reading the perfect novel, a state enhanced considerably by the thought of Hopkins in the role of Stevens, the aging, dignified butler in one of England's grand but fading houses.

Ishiguro, who after three novels has already been hailed as "one of the leading figures in the new generation of British novelists," might seem an unlikely successor to Forster in the Merchant-Ivory corpus. He was born in Nagasaki, Japan, in 1954 and moved as a child to England. Ishiguro's parents initially assumed their move to England would be temporary (his father worked in oil exploration in the North Sea) but they remained, and gave their son what he describes as a "very typical . . . southern English upbringing," although only Japanese was spoken at home.

Majid Tehranian, director of a peace institute in Honolulu, who was born in Iran but is now an American citizen, spoke to a church communications conference recently in New York and made a point that is pertinent to the quest for the perfect novel. All of us live with three kinds of lies, Tehranian said: the lies we tell others, the lies we tell ourselves, and the lies we don't even know we are telling, or more accurately, living.

We know the lies we tell to others; the lies we tell to ourselves are a bit harder to discern; but the only way really to grasp the lies we don't even know we are living is to get outside our own cultural setting. Tehranian cites the old line of the baby fish to the mother fish: "When am I going to see this water you talk about so much?"

A bicultural, bilingual author, Ishiguro displays in *The Remains of the Day* strong powers of observation, coupled with a remarkable grasp of the language that would be spoken or written by his narrator, Stevens, a butler for more than 35 years at Darlington Hall.

Ishiguro takes the reader with Stevens on a six-day ride in July 1956 through the south of England, describing the early morning mists, the pleasant, green countryside, and the modest inns and homes in which he stays. During this period Stevens recalls his career in the service of Lord Darlington.

The opening lines of Stevens's narration immediately draw the reader into the story Ishiguro intends to tell, introducing the voice of a very proper, disciplined butler who knows his place and who lives only to perform his duties. "It seems increasingly likely that I really will undertake the expedition that has been preoccupying my imagination now for some days. An expedition, I should say, which I will undertake alone, in the comfort of Mr. Farraday's Ford; an expedition which, as I foresee it, will take me through much of the finest countryside of England to the West Country, and may keep me away from Darlington Hall for as much as five or six days."

Stevens is motivated to take this journey in part because his new master, an American named Farraday, proposes that he take some time off, and partly because he has just received a letter from Miss Kenton, a former housekeeper who departed the house more than 20 years ago. It is possible, Stevens, surmises, that Miss Kenton might be interested in returning to work at Darlington Hall, since her letter suggests that her marriage has ended. With this hope of adding a veteran housekeeper to the staff—nothing of a more personal nature, of course—Stevens sets off "through the pleasant countryside," with a visit with Miss Kenton as the culmination of his journey.

It is easy to imagine Hopkins in this role, especially after his performance as Henry Wilcox, the rigid symbol of England's upper class, "living comfortably on a lie," as one reviewer puts it. For *The Remains of the Day* is the diary of a man totally unaware of his inner life. Stevens faithfully records his exchanges with Miss Kenton, Lord Darlington, and others who come to the house. We know of his grief over the death of his father only because he recalls someone commenting that he is crying as he continues to perform his duties. Stevens has reached the end of his active life, and he now faces retirement—what a man he meets describes as "the remains of the day." Stevens faces this prospect with no sense that he can relate to people other than as a working butler.

What makes this novel approach perfection—and two comments

on the book jacket actually employ the word—is the way Ishiguro leads the reader into Stevens's life through his own words, enabling us to feel his pride in being a "great" butler and at the same time experience the pain of personal loss which he is utterly unable to acknowledge. Ishiguro has said, "What I'm interested in is not the actual fact that my characters have done things they later regret. I'm interested in how they come to terms with it."

Stevens's relationship with Miss Kenton, which she understands far better than he ever could, is the centerpiece of the book. Not that he ever acknowledges any regret over the pattern the relationship took, but that he needs to "come to terms with it." Stevens's role as a participant in British history—Germany's ambassador to Great Britain was a guest at Darlington Hall for some critical prewar meetings—was, like his relationship with Miss Kenton, something to observe, not to feel.

At the end of his narrative Stevens has to confront the reality of his own "remains of the day." As he looks back, he considers his life through the mists of his self-deception, of which he seems hardly aware. Speaking of Lord Darlington, he says that his employer "wasn't a bad man at all. And at least he had the privilege of being able to say at the end of his life that he made his own mistakes . . . He chose a certain path in life, it proved to be a misguided one, but there, he chose it, he can say that at least. As for myself, I cannot even claim that. You see, I trusted. I trusted in his lordship's wisdom. All those years I served him, I trusted that I was doing something worthwhile. I can't even say I made my own mistakes. Really—one has to ask oneself—what dignity is there in that?"

What dignity, indeed, in not choosing one's own life, but living always outside of it, fixed only on duty and performance. The journey with Stevens is more than a ride through the pleasant countryside of southern England; it is a journey toward one's own "remains of the day."

NO SENSE OF THE SACRED

If you doubt that modern culture has lost a sense of the sacred, consider Steve Martin's latest video release, *A Simple Twist of Fate*. My first viewing of the film was on an overseas flight, which meant that I paid only casual attention. But in the final reel it became apparent that something was seriously wrong. The credits clarified the problem with the revelation that the film is based on George Eliot's novel *Silas Marner*.

Though a favorite assignment in high school English classes, *Silas Marner* resonates best with adult readers who can appreciate Eliot's 19th-century moral and religious worldview. In his attempt to transplant Eliot's story to the contemporary scene—and to avoid, perhaps, anything high school students might find boring—Martin winds up ignoring the religious sensibility that shapes the novel. Though in revolt against established Christianity, Eliot's writing is suffused with Christian symbolism and ideas. She is sympathetic with the emerging Methodist movement (a major character in Eliot's *Adam Bede* is a female Methodist preacher), and relies on John Bunyan's *Pilgrim's Progress* in portraying the struggles of a believer. Moreover, the overall theme in *Silas Marner* is the redemptive power of love.

The novel is a carefully crafted portrayal of a lonely bachelor who raises a child after she wanders into his cabin. Local villagers agree that Silas Marner can keep his miraculous gift after he insists, "The mother's dead, and I reckon it's got no father; it's a lone thing—and I'm a lone thing. My money's gone, I don't know where—and this is come from I don't know where. I know nothing—I'm partly mazed."

Eliot presumed a religious understanding among her readers. Silas gives his daughter his mother's name, Hephzibah, which comes from the Old Testament. The name means "my delight in her," and it is the prophet Isaiah's new name for Jerusalem. Martin changes the name to Mathilda. Eliot's narrative and dialogue are filled with biblical and ecclesiastical images. Which raises the question: How can public school English teachers avoid exploring such references—or the worldview of a writer who wrote (in an earlier novel): "There was a divine work to be done in life, a rule of goodness higher than the opinion of their neighbors; and if the notion of a heaven in reserve for themselves was a little too prominent, yet the theory of fitness for that heaven consisted in purity of heart, in Christ-like compassion in the subduing of selfish desires."

Silas Marner begins when the small religious sect to which Silas belongs unjustly accuses him of stealing, the proof of which is determined by the biblical practice of casting lots. Despondent, Marner moves to another community, where people accept his presence because he is a particularly skilled weaver. At one point, a friendly parishioner of the nearby church, Dolly Winthrop, visits Marner and takes him some of her lard-cakes.

"There's letters pricked on 'em," said Dolly. "I can't read 'em myself, and there's nobody, not Mr. Macey himself, rightly knows what they mean; but they've a good meaning, for they're the same as is on the pulpit cloth at church . . . whativer the letters are, they'v a good meaning; and it's a stamp as has been in our house, Ben says, ever since he was a little un, and his mother used to put it on cakes, and I've allays put it on too; for if there's any good, we've need of it i' this world."

"It's I.H.S.," said Silas . . . [who] was as unable to interpret the letters as Dolly, but there was no possibility of misunderstanding the desire to give comfort that made itself heard in her quiet tones."

In discussing this passage in *Silas Marner: Memory and Salvation*, Patrick Swinden notes: "This aspect of a more ritualistic religion than his own (the letters are a monogram representing a contraction of the Greek spelling of 'Jesus') makes no impression on him." The conversation between Marner and Dolly becomes a primer on the difference between the views of a sect and Dolly's more "high church" practices. Silas says he has never been to "church"; he has attended a "chapel," and he knows nothing of infant baptism, since his tradition believes in immersion. But none of this exchange on religious practices makes it into Steve Martin's film.

With the disappearance of the sacred from modern culture, any adaptation of religiously oriented works is inevitably truncated. I was alerted to another instance of this problem in film through a conversation at the Berlin Film Festival. We were discussing the closing section of Krzysztof Kieslowski's *Blue*, the first part of his *Three Colors* trilogy. (*Red*, the third in the trilogy, has earned the Polish-born Kieslowski an Academy Award nomination for best director.) In *Blue*, Julie, the widow of a famous European composer, joins with a colleague to complete an oratorio that her husband had begun before dying in a car crash. She opens a book, points to a biblical passage and says, "In Greek the rhythm is different." A few moments later the film concludes with the oratorio played and sung on the sound track as the camera focuses on individuals Julie has met and helped earlier in the film. The oratorio is sung in Greek. The word "agape" is repeated several times.

My friend pointed out that the film's original English subtitles scroll the text from 1 Corinthians 13 across the bottom of the screen, concluding with the passage, "The greatest of these is love." But when *Blue* was distributed in the U.S. by Miramax, the subtitles for the words of the oratorio were removed in both the large-screen and video versions. Unless the viewer understands Greek, the fact that the film closes with a celebratory rendering of 1 Corinthians 13 is lost. When my friend asked a representative of Miramax what happened to the subtitles, he was told they were deleted so as not to confuse the American audience.

Kieslowski began his filmmaking career with a ten-part series on the Decalogue. His films are filled with scriptural and spiritual references. *New York Post* critic David Kehr, a writer who understands Kieslowski's spirituality, observed in *Film Comment*: "One shouldn't be surprised to find biblical allusions in the work of a man who has filmed the Ten Commandments." The theme of redemption as a gift that the sinner does not fully comprehend is central to Kieslowski's work. Kehr concludes: "In each of the three films of the trilogy, a betrayal leads to a sense of larger understanding. . . . Three films that seemed to have been carefully distinguished by tone, content and appearance turn out to be the same film, telling the same story of alienation overcome, loneliness dissolved in human warmth, isolation subsumed by a sense of infinite interdependence."

Director Arthur Penn recalled recently his experience with his 1965 film, *Mickey One*, which was to have been the first of a series of pictures that would be "different" from mainstream commercial products. In a secular context, *Mickey One* asks the question, read in a stammer by a storefront preacher, "Is there any word from the Lord?" The film closes with Warren Beatty, as a nightclub performer on stage, looking up into a blinding spotlight, asking, "Is there anyone up there?" *Mickey One* was a daring experiment; secular critics were intrigued; religious critics were elated. But the film was a commercial failure. Perhaps it was "too confusing." No other films in the series were made. Such is the burden and the challenge of making movies in a desacralized culture.

CONTROL AS ORIGINAL SIN

It isn't until several days after the accident that Lottie lets herself—makes herself—think about it. Think about how it was for all of them, for Cameron and Elizabeth, and for Jessica." The opening paragraph of Sue Miller's novel *For Love* hints at the answer to the novel's central question: "Where are the 20th-century love stories?" Her answer: "They're not allowed." And why are they not allowed? Miller never explicitly answers this question, but her story testifies to the shallowness of modern love and of couples afraid to make the leap of faith into commitment and trust. Unable to give up control, says Miller, modern lovers settle for sex, passing infatuations, boring marriages.

Miller's novel, for me her best and most mature, explores the interlocking lives of a small group of friends. The accident that Lottie wills herself to put out of mind and then recall is the novel's central event, the moment when everyone's personal control is temporarily erased. Jessica, a young woman who works as an au pair for Elizabeth, is accidentally killed by Lottie's brother, Cameron. He is driving at night in the rain to confront Elizabeth, the woman he thinks he loves. Distracted by his worry over Elizabeth's phone call informing him that she will return to her husband, Cameron does not see Jessica until she steps directly into the path of his car. It is an accident—but nevertheless Cameron was distracted, and he was driving the car. He must share responsibility for the accident.

Elizabeth also shares some of the blame; she initiated the affair with Cameron, and she sent Jessica out to intercept Cameron. Lottie knows that she, too, bears some of the blame because she made the suggestion that led to the fateful summer affair between Elizabeth and Cameron. In Miller's universe there are those who know they are responsible for their actions, and there are those so lost that they deny responsibility for anything. These are, in effect, hardened sinners and repentant sinners.

Lottie, the book's narrator, reports her experience with both types of sinners, and it is upon her own growth from hardened to repentant sinner that the book is built. As the novel begins, Lottie has returned to Boston from a troubled marriage to prepare her mother's house for sale. Her 20-year-old son Ryan joins her to work on the house, and his presence sets up a familiar Miller situation: a mother struggling simultaneously with her roles as parent and daughter. Miller builds her narrative around physical, sweaty work on the house, a growing intimacy between Lottie and Elizabeth during coffee-break conversations, and Lottie's discovery that her brother's obsession is being exploited by Elizabeth to fill her lonely summer months.

Miller, a disciplined novelist, reports only what Lottie sees or hears—including an ingenious use of recorded telephone messages. Control is an absolute necessity for Lottie. It is her way of dealing with a sorrow begun in a loveless childhood (her father went to jail for fraud, adding to her sense of uncertainty). Lottie wills herself to deal with problems only when she can no longer put them aside. She now recalls painfully that as a child she was programmed to fail by her alcoholic mother (Cameron was to be the successful child).

Bruised by her first marriage—to Derek, Ryan's father—Lottie has an affair with Jack, a romantic fling made possible because Jack's wife has suffered several debilitating strokes. The wife dies, and Jack and Lottie marry; reality intrudes, and Lottie runs away. These details have the flavor of a soap opera, but through them Miller probes the nature of love (a topic that Lottie, a free-lance author, is researching). With a superb realist style and sensitivity to relations between men and women, Miller explores her insight that intimacy cannot survive in an atmosphere that emphasizes control.

The control/trust dilemma implicit in Miller's story might be described in Christian terms as original sin—the absence of trust in others and in God. Miller (whose father, Jim Nichols, taught church history at several Protestant seminaries) does not employ such theological categories. But her novels suggest them, and they also indicate—as in Lottie's final journey—that original sin need not have the final word.

Each of Miller's three novels focuses on a family in trouble. In *The Good Mother* a family is disturbed by an ambiguous encounter between a child and a mother's lover. In *Family Pictures* a retarded child, who the mother insists must remain at home, exercises control over a family.

Lottie's research on love leads her to John Donne, an encounter Miller describes with her lean and evocative attention to physical detail: "One night—this was about ten days before the accident—she was reading Donne's love poetry. Just a few of them before she dropped off to sleep, she told herself. She was propped up in bed, and the circle of light fell on the worn white sheets and across the yellowed pages of the old book. A musty smell rose from it as Lottie turned the pages, a smell that weighted the words with physical meaning for her. 'For, not in nothing, nor in things/Extreme, and scattering bright,' she read, 'can love inhere.'"

Lottie moves finally toward a moment of catharsis in which, after confronting her brother with his destructive, possessive love for Elizabeth, she begins a long trip alone. She has begun to sense, with Donne, that love is not going to inhere in "things," and she has made a decision to start life anew. The journey is undertaken with the added burden of a severe toothache which Lottie tries to ignore, relying for relief on strong pills. This becomes a memorable metaphor, written in Miller's precise physical style, of a person denying reality.

As in her earlier novels, Miller eschews a conventional happy ending. Her characters descend too far into pain and conflict for easy conclusions. They must settle instead for new beginnings built on broken pieces, which in *For Love* are as diverse as an old house restored and a painful tooth replaced—and as hopeful as a tentative relationship that promises to begin, for a change, with trust.

BEFORE THE BOOK SALE

My town puts on a book sale every fall. Proceeds go to a worthy cause, and I am told that the event is well attended. I never go because I already have too many books on my crowded shelves. But I do participate in the sale as a supplier. It is for this reason that each summer as the time to turn books in approaches I am seized by an intense feeling of anxiety. I know I have to prune my shelves, and I also know that there is no reason to hold on to all the books I have. As I choose what goes and what stays, I confront my mortality—who will want all these books when I am gone?—and my past. Each title evokes a memory of an earlier time of intense interest in a particular topic. What has happened to that passion? What was behind the decision to keep one title and reject others? And when I reject a book I once thought had to remain with me forever, I wonder in what ways I've changed. Weeding out books is a painful process that demands personal clarity.

I found some reassurance recently when I came across a quote from Henry Adams, who once described himself as "aching to absorb knowledge, and helpless to find it." This hunger to know more, and the sense of frustration when more turns out not to be enough, is no doubt a factor in our acquisition of books. Loyalties are developed over time as writers are invited into one's life. I'm not entirely sure why some books are favored and others never make the cut, but I do know that the writers who elicit my deepest loyalty are those who connect layers of meaning, who link insight and information in surprising ways.

I found the quote from Adams in a *New Yorker* review of *Panama*, a new novel by Eric Zencey, which puts the American writer Henry Adams in a fictional situation—"sniffling around Paris in 1892," searching for a young American painter with an interest in architecture. Adams is one author who remains a permanent resident on my shelf, never to be sent into book-sale oblivion. He had an intense curiosity about so many things that I wish I knew more about. Zencey knows this side of Adams, which is what must have led him to imagine Adams as a detective, trying to find a woman whose disappearance is related to the financial scandals surrounding the building of the Panama Canal.

Adams would indeed have wanted to know more about the financial scandals that tainted the canal project. He would also have been fascinated by a venture that transformed world commerce. He would view the canal as part of the new technology, the great leap forward which he described with both dread and excitement in the chapter titled "The Virgin and the Dynamo" in *The Education of Henry Adams*. For Adams, industrialization was a decidedly mixed blessing, but he still needed to know all he could about it. Stephen Schiff, who wrote the *New Yorker* review, points out that Adams's ache for knowledge accords well with the role of detective, for "what propels the great fictional detectives—and the people who love to read about them—is something very like Adams's epistemological ache."

Books by and about Adams must remain on my shelf. Who gets jettisoned? As I toss one book into the discard sack and leave another in its familiar spot, I begin to see a pattern. The authors I like to keep around are those with a flair for connections, who, like Adams, possess an intellectual hunger that is conveyed through the sensibility of a Poet or a Prophet. Gail Godwin describes this quality in *The Good Husband*:

> We live within a dense tissue of correspondences. They connect all the levels of our existence, whether we recognize the fact or not. The difference between your Miss or Mr. Literal-mind and the Prophet/Poet is simply this: To Miss Literal-mind, a seed is a seed. She shakes it out of its Burpee packet, covers it with dirt, waters it faithfully, and achieves her petunia. That's all she aspired to: a petunia. And when Mr. Literal-mind lowers his face into the lush heart of a rose, he sees and smells what he expected to see and smell: a rose. If by chance he spies a worm nestled in its innermost folds, he dusts it with pest powder and that's that, his job is done.
>
> But when our Prophet considers the lowly mustard seed, what he sees is the growth process of the human spirit: how

a tiny insignificant beginning can grow into a luxuriant shrub capable of sheltering others. And when our Poet contemplates the Sick Rose, he sees beyond mere plant pathology: for him the rose's enfolding of the battening intruder is a powerful image of human sexual love with its inevitable fate of decay and death.

There is no way I could keep all of the Poets and Prophets on the shelf, but certain writers must be retained, kept close by for that crucial moment when a connection must be made, a light lit amid the darkness. With that understanding, the pruning becomes easier. Still, I wonder about the future home of the books I send away. It may be that one reader's Literal-mind will be another reader's Poet or Prophet, and that those who rummage through my discarded books will find a special word of connection.

AMONG THE LILIES

For the Reverend Clarence Arthur Wilmot, the loss of faith was accompanied by a distinct sensation: "a visceral surrender, a set of dark sparkling bubbles escaping upward." The Presbyterian minister "was standing, at the moment of the ruinous pang, on the first floor of the rectory, wondering if in view of the heat he might remove his black serge jacket, since no visitor was scheduled to call until after dinnertime, when the Church Building Requirements Committee would arrive to torment him with its ambitions."

Thus does John Updike report on Wilmot's abrupt and irreversible deconversion experience at the outset of *In the Beauty of the Lilies*, a four-generation saga which is partly a fictional version of Updike's family history, partly an account of the decline of religious faith in America, and partly a reflection of Updike's own angry, personal struggle to find religious meaning.

Those who have followed Updike's multilayered theological struggles since his first novel, *Poorhouse Fair* in 1959, will find Updike at his best in *Lilies*. He describes with poetic precision characters whose actions provoke the reader to beg them to choose another path; writes dialogue that reveals the pain brought on by false moves; and creates images with painterlike acuity. Here, for example, is the faithless Wilmot: "a tall, narrow-chested man of forty-four, with a drooping sand-colored mustache and a certain afterglow of masculine beauty, despite a vague look of sluggish unhealth."

In his memoir *Self-Consciousness*, Updike refers to the phrase from the "Battle Hymn of the Republic" that supplies the title, "In the beauty of the lilies, Christ was born across the sea," as "an odd and uplifting line" that "seems to me to summarize what I had to say about America." He told *Publishers Weekly* that in this novel "he has attempted 'to make God a character,' although in ways that illuminate spiritual emptiness in American life."

With his loss of his faith and his career in ministry, Wilmot begins a terrible downward plunge that reduces his family to near poverty. His voice leaves him in the middle of a sermon as he argues for a theology he does not believe. His wife rushes forward to finish the sermon. Later, much to the horror of his wife, who enjoys the prestige of her husband's profession, he confesses to his church session that he is no longer able to preach and must leave his assignment "at the corner of Straight Street and Broadway" (just one of many references to the conflict between God and Mammon).

Before Wilmot can relinquish his post, however, he must confront his ecclesiastical superior, presbytery moderator Thomas Dreaver. "Pale and rounded in feature, with short fair hair brushed away from a central parting, he wore a single-breasted, slate-blue business suit and was businesslike in manner, save for an extra smoothness, a honeyed promissory timbre to his voice that marked him as an executive of Christian business." Such a man cannot understand why Wilmot's belief that "the God of the Pentateuch was an absurd bully, barbarically thundering through a cosmos entirely misconceived," would cause him to leave the ministry. "Relativity is what we must live by now," says Dreaver. "Everything is relative, and what matters is how we, we human creatures, relate to one another."

Dreaver argues that Wilmot's lack of faith should be viewed as but a momentary blip on the path of a career of considerable promise in a prosperous institution that does good for others and rewards its clergy handsomely. The modern church knows how to adapt:

> Think of how our two seminaries relate to their surroundings—Union in the middle of the nation's biggest city and from the most savory part of Manhattan at that, but drawing vitality and the pulse of reality from it. Princeton sitting down there in fox-hunting country, surrounded by estates and lettuce farms, cut off from the real, urban, industrial world. . . . Change, Mr. Wilmot—from the nebulae to the microbes change is the way of Creation, and it must be our way, but for God's sake don't destroy your essential self. Don't give up your calling. I promise you, there is nothing in your beliefs or unbeliefs that can't serve as the basis for an effective and deeply satisfying Christian ministry.

Wilmot is not persuaded, and soon is trudging door to door selling encyclopedias. Before long he is dead of tuberculosis, leaving behind a family destined to search for an alternative to the faith that Wilmot lost on that hot July afternoon.

In *Self-Consciousness*, Updike describes his grandfather, Harley Updike, as a man who left the ministry because of what his 1923 obituary called "a throat affection." The story of his grandfather, Updike told *Publishers Weekly*, became "part of family mythology, a kind of blot on the common vitality of the Updike clan." It also became the germ of this novel.

Updike links Wilmot's loss of faith to the rise of movies. At the exact moment that Wilmot gives up on God, Mary Pickford faints while making a film under the direction of D. W. Griffith. These two famous names from the era of silent films are invoked to suggest that the movie industry fills the void left by an absent deity. Hollywood is the new repository of values, and its stars provide the models of behavior.

It turns out, then, that Wilmot's granddaughter becomes a movie star who personifies this modern idol-making institution. Alma DeMott gains fame because she knows how to play the game, and has no scruples. Alma stutters under pressure (a trait she shares with Updike himself), but she rises above this flaw and is a huge success playing opposite such stars as Clark Gable, Gary Cooper and William Holden. There is an emptiness to her success, however—a void that cannot be filled by a succession of lovers, marriage into wealth, or worldwide acclaim. (If, as the clues suggest, Alma is the Updike figure in the novel, he is being unusually hard on himself.)

Alma's son joins a Colorado religious commune which bursts into public view in a Waco-like confrontation. She rushes to the site and, not incidentally, conducts frequent press conferences, simultaneously grieving over her child while being acutely conscious of the camera angles. Updike does not appear to care for Hollywood. Several of his novels have been made into movies, none successfully. Neither his metaphorical, poetic style nor his theological probing is the stuff that Hollywood likes to shape into box-office successes.

What are we to make of Updike's saga of faith lost and never found? It is possible that our most revered God-searching Protestant author-theologian is suggesting that he would trade all his best sellers and public acclaim for the chance to go back and tell Clarence Wilmot that God is still here and wants to be in touch. It's also possible he is saying that we cannot begin to locate the God that Wilmot lost until we confess that there is no substitute for belief in the Christ who was born "across the sea, with a glory in his bosom that transfigures you and me."

SOMETHING OF SUBSTANCE

My early memories of reading fall into two categories. The dark memory is of Miss Drew's first grade classroom, where I struggled to decipher the letters that described Dick and Jane running. The brighter memory is of a backyard tree with limbs strong enough to climb and foliage thick enough to keep away prying eyes. That was where I read library books through long summer afternoons. It is that brighter memory that led me to join my local library board and led, in turn, to my attendance at a recent meeting of the Public Library Association.

The convention featured speeches and workshops and above all commercial exhibits—of books, furniture, and what seemed like acres of computer equipment designed to bring libraries into the modern world of cyberspace. Though I was impressed by all the online equipment, it gave me a chill. I know we need computers to link us to the Internet and the Worldwide Web, but the computer by itself is only a linkage device, and the new technology can be a vehicle for the further commercialization of society.

On the way back from the library meeting, I read an article in *Harper's* by novelist Jonathan Franzen which describes the disappearance of the "social novel" in American literature—that genre characterized by in-depth "reporting" presented through a narrative. With a few exceptions—Franzen cites the work of John Updike and Toni Morrison—novels today tell stories that are shallow, predictable, and designed to soothe, distract, excite. Most of all, they are designed to sell.

Franzen argues that these novels reflect a market ideology. How commercially driven is our culture? Consider the Atlanta Olympics, supposedly a tribute to amateurism. Sponsor identification competed with the athletes for viewer attention.

The news media are also captive to market forces, and are attuned to the stories that sell. Compare the number of inches devoted to covering sports and entertainment to that given to more serious topics. And as movie advertising increases, so has the space devoted to popular reporting on movie stars and directors. Franzen writes: "As the associate publisher of the *Orange County Register* said to a *New York Times* reporter in 1994: 'Why do we keep deceiving ourselves about what a newspaper really is? Why do we keep deceiving ourselves about the role of editor as marketer?'"

Flannery O'Connor observed that the business of fiction is to "embody mystery through manners." Franzen explains O'Connor's terms this way: mystery is "how human beings avoid or confront the meaning of existence"; manners are "the nuts and bolts of how human beings behave." He argues that consumerism seeks to render both mystery and manners "moot," replacing them with predictable descriptions of a "commercial generality" that reaches the widest possible audience with little or no concern for either "the meaning of existence" or the way people live.

In his bleak study of popular culture, Franzen encountered a soulmate in Shirley Brice Heath, a professor of English and linguistics at Stanford who has been examining American reading habits. Heath has concluded that the habit of reading "substantive material" is something a child learns from the example of one or both parents. In addition, writes Franzen, young readers need to find a person "with whom they can share their interest."

Heath confirmed for Franzen the moral significance of reading good fiction in a consumer society. "Again and again, readers told Heath the same thing: 'Reading enables me to maintain a sense of something substantive—my ethical integrity, my intellectual integrity.'" She found that substantive works of fiction offered people "the only places where there was some vivid, public hope of coming to grips with the ethical, philosophical, and sociopolitical dimensions of life that were elsewhere treated so simplistically. From Agamemnon forward, for example, we've been having to deal with the conflict between loyalty to one's family and loyalty to the state. And strong works of fiction are what refuse to give easy answers to the conflict, to paint things as black and white, good guys versus bad guys. They're everything that pop psychology is not." Heath adds that "reading good fiction is like reading a particularly rich section of a religious text. What religion and good fiction have in common is that the answers aren't there, there isn't closure."

Substantive fiction protects the reader against the deadening impact of commercial society. Novelists of this sort are "preserving a tradition of precise, expressive language; a habit of looking past surfaces into interiors; maybe an understanding of private experience and public context as distinct but interpenetrating; maybe mystery, maybe manners. Above all, they are preserving a community of readers and writers, and the way in which members of this community recognize each other is that nothing in the world seems simple to them."

Popular culture wants quick answers and obvious plots. And commerce abhors openness. Ever try to leave a car salesroom without closing the deal? You are warned that "this offer expires at 5 P.M. and the boss won't let me renew it ever again." The next time that happens, tell the salesperson that "these are the best of times and the worst of times," and that you don't plan on closing a sale tonight.

Commerce is essential to society, but it must remain our servant, not our master. We need to wire up the libraries and bring on the computers. But they won't help us much unless they lead us into and not away from mystery and manners.

RELIGION
IN PUBLIC DISCOURSE

"May we not justly fear that the awful calamity of Civil War, which now desolates the land, may be but a punishment, inflicted on us, for our presumptuous sins, to the needful end of our national reformation as a whole People? . . . It behooves us then, to humble ourselves before the offended Power, to confess our national sins, and to pray for clemency and forgiveness."

Abraham Lincoln

JEWS AND CHRISTIANS: A DIFFERENT SCENARIO

I rving Kristol is an author, the publisher of *National Interest* and the coeditor of the *Public Interest*. In the manner of fellow neo-conservatives Richard John Neuhaus and Michael Novak, Kristol tends to have much greater confidence in the American Way than the biblical prophetic tradition permits. But to their credit, these three have consistently stood as enemies of secularism, the dominant faith of our culture. Kristol has recently stirred up considerable debate among his fellow Jews because he has had the audacity to write that American Jewry might benefit from a "revived Christianity" at the center of American culture.

Writing in a recent issue of *Commentary* (published by the American Jewish Committee), Kristol says that secular humanism has not been good for this country and also has not been "good for the Jews." For a people who have known pogroms, the Holocaust and both virulent and subtle anti-Semitism, the phrase "good for the Jews" is not a casual one. The phrase is most often used today as a humorous aside, but as one Jewish acquaintance of mine pointed out, to his Lithuanian grandparents a knock on the door could be "bad for the Jews" if the visitor were a policeman.

Kristol considers what is good for the Jews as he traces the rise of secularization and the triumph of a new "religious" impulse over "the traditional biblical religions that formed the framework of Western civilization." This victorious worldview, he adds, is "named, fairly and accurately, secular humanism." While no self-respecting secular humanist would use the term "religion" to describe this enlightened, "modern scientific view of the universe," it is a religion nonetheless, for it makes inferences that are "metaphysical, and in the end theological."

Secular humanism gives lip service to the role of religious tradition while insisting that religion remain mute in public discourse. Alan Dershowitz, in his angry, abrasive and at times amusing book *Chutzpah*, argues for a more aggressive Jewish presence in American culture to defend American culture against all "religious" incursions that threaten Jewish identity. Dershowitz cherishes the faith of his parents and honors the high holy days even as he proudly insists that he is a secular Jew—thus leaving unanswered the question that bothers religious Jews: what happens to biblically based Judaism if every Jew follows Dershowitz's example?

Secularism that honors religious tradition even as it rejects it troubles Kristol, who sums up the dominant Western worldview for both Jews and Christians in one phrase, "Man makes himself. That is to say, the universe is bereft of transcendental meaning, it has no inherent teleology, and it is within the power of humanity to comprehend natural phenomena and to control and manipulate them so as to improve the human estate."

Our "immortal souls" are victims of progress, replaced by the temporal "self," which is served by science, literature and psychology, all of which, says Kristol, operate today "without benefit of what, in traditional terms, was regarded as a religious dimension." People still go to church or synagogue, but "very few educated people actually think that their immortal souls are at stake as a result of their beliefs or actions."

Secular humanism had an impact on European Jews that was "far more striking than among Christians." This was true largely because Jews needed emancipation and civic equality, Kristol says. Society-shaping "prophetic Judaism" gradually pushed aside the more spiritually oriented "rabbinic Judaism." The result was that the majority of Jewish immigrants to America, convinced by their European experience that equality and freedom of opportunity would be their salvation in the new land, entered life here as committed liberals. Even those who practiced their faith supported secular humanism because "it has assured them of an unparalleled degree of comfort and security." Which explains, Kristol argues, why American Jews are so vigilant about any signs of traditional religion in the public square.

But this determination to keep religion locked in the private sphere is not good for the Jews, Kristol contends. "The greatest single threat to the Jewish community today is not anti-Semitism but intermarriage, at a 30-40 percent rate. In spite of fervent and frequent admonitions from Reform and Conservative rabbis, ancestral piety is of less value to younger liberal Jews today than their commitment to modern rationalism. In this they mirror their Christian counterparts for whom religious holy days are occasions for warm, cozy memories, not renewed moral commitments."

Our secular society is on the verge of a dramatic change, Kristol says. Even as it dominates institutions in our society—schools, courts, churches, media—secular humanism has begun to lose its credibility because it has two fundamental flaws. The first is the lack of any foundation for its future. Secular humanism offers a statement of "the necessary assumption of a moral code, but it cannot deliver any such code itself." One accepts a moral code on faith—the faith that "one's ancestors . . . were not fools and that we have much to learn from them and their experience. Pure reason can offer a critique of moral beliefs but it cannot engender them."

The second flaw of secular humanism is its failure to provide meaning. No community can survive, Kristol points out, "if it is persuaded—or even if it suspects—that its members are leading meaningless lives in a meaningless universe." The history of Western thought testifies that secular humanism has failed to recognize and then subdue meaninglessness.

In *Continental Drift*, novelist Russell Banks captures some of this meaninglessness in the character of Bob Dubois, a 30-year-old oil burner repairman. "His wife Elaine loves and admires him, his daughters Ruthie and Emma practically worship him, his boss, Fred Turner, says he needs him and his friends think he has a good sense of humor. . . . He votes Democratic, as his father did, goes occasionally to mass with his wife and children and believes in God the way he believes in politicians—he knows He exists but doesn't depend on him for anything. He loves his wife and children. He has a girlfriend. He hates his life."

What will fill the spiritual void of people like Bob Dubois? Contemporary media—locked into their secularist mode—answer by reporting on the worship of "Mother Earth" by environmentalists or on the rise in New Age spirituality. Kristol sees something more significant happening: the resurgence of traditional religion to play "a more central role in American life."

Since the majority of Americans are Christian in background, Kristol assumes that Christianity is the tradition most likely to fill the void. As responses to his article have already indicated, secular Jews are horrified at the prospect. But Kristol insists that religious Judaism has a far better future under a society shaped by Christian sensibility than it would under any upsurge in "anti-biblical barbarism that will challenge Christianity, Judaism, and Western civilization altogether."

Kristol comments, "One does get the impression that many American Jews would rather see Judaism vanish through intermarriage than have the President say something nice about Jesus Christ." Such Jews forget, says Kristol, that "it was the pagans—the Babylonians and the Romans—who destroyed the temples and twice imposed exile on the Jewish people."

Kristol does not think a "less secular, more religious society will mean an increase in anti-Semitism." Jews are firmly established in the mainstream of American life, and opinion polls indicate that most Americans "display little paranoid distrust of Jews, and in fact are less interested in them than most Jews imagine."

Recounting the debate stirred by the *Commentary* article, J. J. Goldberg observes that most Conservative and Reform Jews believe Jewish rights "depend on a secular society," and that any rebirth of religiosity poses a serious threat to those rights. Goldberg asked *Commentary* editor Norman Podhoretz about Kristol's article, and quoted Podhoretz as saying about Kristol: "I'm not sure he's right about the rise of the Christian right. I'm not big on predicting the future myself" (*Jerusalem Report*).

Kristol's article made no reference to the "Christian right," however, so it occurred to me that Podhoretz might have been misquoted. Hearing the word "Christian," Goldberg may simply have assumed that the topic was the "Christian right"—a common fault among journalists. I asked Podhoretz if he had been misquoted. Yes, he told me; in his interview with Goldberg he had made no reference to any single programmatic manifestation of Christianity.

It is understandable that a journalist contemplating a "revived Christianity" would sense the specter of the "Christian right"—a group with a fixed moralistic formula for reshaping society. But a revived Christianity does not necessarily mean the assertion of a specific program to fill the social void left by the god that failed. Kristol's own scenario at least suggests the possibility—and the challenge—of a revived Christianity playing a central role in a pluralistic culture, helping shape a future that will be good for the Jews and for all segments of our society.

REVERENCE AND THE FREEDOM TO REVISE

In an effort to make sense of the presidential campaign, I turned to journalist James Reston's recent autobiography, *Deadline*, thinking that his insights into earlier campaigns might put the 1992 race into perspective. What I found was not horse-race data about the past but a definition of wisdom taken from Alfred North Whitehead. "It is the first step in wisdom," Whitehead wrote in *Symbolism*, "to recognize that the major advances in civilization are processes which all but wreck the society in which they occur. . . . The art of free society consists, first, in the maintenance of the symbolic code, and secondly, in fearlessness of revision. Those societies which cannot combine reverence for their symbols with freedom of revision must ultimately decay from anarchy or from slow atrophy."

A presidential campaign is, ideally, a time for reassessing where we are as a people—a quadrennial exercise in pulse-taking and planning. Our best leaders are those who challenge us to recall "the symbolic code" that brought us to this moment and that enables us to confront the "major advances" that threaten to undermine us.

Abraham Lincoln responded to perhaps our most traumatic social shift by eloquently calling upon our symbolic code. He did not trivialize the code for his own partisan purposes, but rather reminded people of their common bond. Lincoln possessed a religious sensibility appropriate to a pluralistic culture. He spoke a biblical and democratic language that could rally the nation to look beyond the anger and suffering brought on by civil war. In the midst of a war that had divided the nation, he called upon Americans to remember the moral center that formed their union. He appealed to what was best in their tradition.

In calling for a national day of prayer during the war, Lincoln wrote: "We have been the recipients of the choicest bounties of heaven. We have been preserved, these many years, in peace and prosperity. We have grown in numbers, wealth and power, as no other nation has grown. But we have forgotten God. We have forgotten the gracious hand which preserved us in peace, and multiplied and enriched and strengthened us; and we have vainly imagined . . . that all these blessings were produced by some superior wisdom and virtue of our own. Intoxicated with unbroken success, we have become too self-sufficient to feel the necessity of redeeming and preserving grace, too proud to pray to the God that made us! It behooves us, then, to humble ourselves before the offended Power, to confess our national sins, and to pray for clemency and forgiveness."

Today, more than a century after Lincoln articulated a moral center on behalf of national reconciliation, secularity has so infiltrated our leadership and our elite institutions that presidential candidates are reluctant to employ moral language and are uncertain about any symbolic code. When they do use such language, they tend to trivialize it. In the 1988 campaign President Bush invoked the American flag in a way that trivialized that symbol, and Michael Dukakis became an object of ridicule by donning a tank-driver's helmet—an ineffective use of an empty symbol of patriotism. In both instances the use of the symbols was demeaning both to the user and to the audience, since they were so obviously calculated political gestures.

When Martin Luther King Jr. helped lead this nation through a nonviolent civil war, he drew upon the language of the black church and on biblical images of hope and reconciliation. This language has been part of our national identity since John Winthrop challenged the Pilgrims to create a new commonwealth, the creation of which demanded a responsibility to others and to God. Winthrop's sermon was a favorite of Ronald Reagan's, but in praising this nation as the "city upon on a hill" Reagan conveniently ignored Winthrop's reminder that with the gift of the new land came the burden of discipline and service and accountability to God.

Martin Luther King spoke in the Winthrop tradition when he called for an end to segregation in the 1960s. He denounced racial separation in language that appealed to our moral center, and thereby he sustained people even as he challenged them. King said, in effect, that we must change our behavior as a people, but that we can do so with the assurance that the change is consistent with God's will and with our deepest commitments as a people.

In recent elections it has become obvious that presidential candidates are welcome to use religious language only in certain communities. Mainline churches, for the most part, have accepted the priority of secular language. They are anxious to keep religious matters separated from political issues.

Only in the black churches and in some white evangelical churches is it acceptable to link God's purposes and demands to social issues as King did. (The Democratic candidates find their way to black churches, the Republicans to conservative white ones.) The "symbolic code" that Whitehead insisted was essential in coping with change is expressed openly only in those religious communities outside the mainstream that is dominated by the secular elite.

The 1990s will be a time of enormous shifts, processes which may "all but wreck the society in which they occur." The person chosen to lead this country into the next decade will have to be sensitive both to the demands of change and to the need to meet that change in the light of the rich symbolic code that has sustained the nation from its beginnings.

THE RELIGIOUS MUSIC WITHOUT THE WORDS

Indianapolis

If it is true, as G. K. Chesterton said, that the U.S. is a nation with the soul of a church, then why is it so difficult to use explicit religious references in public discourse? That question was at the center of a recent conference at which more than 200 people assembled under the auspices of the Center for the Study and Religion and American Culture to discuss "public religious discourse and America's pluralistic society." It would appear, as conference speakers suggested, that this nation's spiritual nature has been forced to hide under a secular shield, its traditional religious rhetoric muted to protect sensibilities in a pluralistic society.

But history is difficult to ignore. Randall Balmer of Columbia University suggested that the most effective oratorical style in contemporary politics is strongly influenced by the evangelical Protestant tradition. The style and cadences of 18th-, 19th- and early 20th-century preaching, with its call for change and its insistence that the world is divided into good and evil, provide the "music" whenever effective political rhetoric is employed.

It is the evangelical preaching tradition, not the high-church tradition emphasizing sacrament and liturgy, that has shaped American communicative style, Balmer argued. This has left us with a political rhetoric that is simplistic, dualistic, populist, and charged with calls to repentance. But it is the style, not the content, that has survived from the nation's initial Protestant worldview.

William F. Buckley once observed that anyone who mentions God more than once at a New York dinner party won't receive another invitation. Specific words from the Christian or Jewish traditions are considered inappropriate in public forums, most participants at this conference acknowledged. Yet such religious "music" is at the core of our society; it is part of who we are as a people. With the arrival of pluralism and the need for tolerance, that music survives only in a denuded form of moral discourse that has little connection with its original source.

In one sense, the music lives in our civil religion—in our celebration of sacred days, sacred places and revered leaders. But the words to the music have lost their rootedness in the ultimate. Drew history professor Leigh Schmidt observed how Christmas celebrations have been secularized. Examining personal diaries, newspaper reports and advertisements from the late 19th and early 20th centuries, Schmidt noted the way Christmas was once celebrated in department stores like Wanamaker's in Philadelphia, which featured hymn-singing and elaborate religious symbolism that turned the store's cathedral-like central area into a commercialized version of a church. Today the emphasis is on non-Christian Christmas symbols. The baby Jesus has given way to Frosty the snowman and Rudolph the red-nosed reindeer.

Pluralism required this shift. Until early in this century Protestants controlled public discourse, leaving minority faiths and people of no faith without a voice. In recognition of these minorities and as an expression of tolerance and openness, the Protestant control has given way to a bland secular voice that offends no one but also fails to provide a religious worldview to help shape public discourse.

Still, as Balmer argues, political rhetoric and cultural style cannot escape their parentage. Consider the style of some of our presidential candidates, who have employed what Balmer describes as the major components of the evangelical preaching tradition: the appearance of spontaneity, a cadence that appears to be leading toward an altar call, the reduction of complex problems to a simple delineation of good versus evil. Ronald Reagan had the style. George Bush does not, though he can approximate it in 30-second sound bites (and did so with devastating effect against Michael Dukakis, one political figure who does not share the evangelical style). Bill Clinton and Jerry Brown both have the style, though in different ways. Clinton can be a preacher who connects with his audience (especially in black churches) through biblical passages. Brown can be the angry prophet denouncing the privileged, a frontier evangelist pointing the finger of condemnation at the sinful establishment.

This Protestant heritage has bequeathed to us, in short, a dualistic and populist style. But now the words are politically correct only if they reject all signs of the Protestant past. At its worst, that past reflected imperialism, patriarchy and exclusivity. At its best it formed the nation's soul and moral core.

Later in its series of conferences the center will solicit papers on the role of the media in shaping the expression of religion in public discourse. But the media issue found its way into these discussions in a paper by Janet Fishburn. Another professor from Drew, Fishburn was a member of the task force that wrote the study on sexuality for the Presbyterian Church (U.S.A.) which was widely debated in the media and at the church's General Assembly. Fishburn said that the task force had tried to use "expressive" language in dealing with sexuality—not sex, as it was invariably termed by the media—but that this language was converted by the secular media into a dualistic, simplistic and moralistic language that treated sexual relationships as if they were being entered on a police docket. As a result the committee's attempt to be pastoral was perceived as an abandonment of traditional moral standards. The committee wanted to deal "expressively" with evolving forms of sexuality, but it did not find the language to do so. It also found little support for its effort within the church, which was not prepared to distinguish between normative moral statements and statements of pastoral care, especially when that nuance was ignored by secular reporters in search of a good story.

Fishburn acknowledges that the committee should have anticipated the outrage the report prompted not only in the church but also in the communications industry, which has assumed the role of guarding national mores, even as it profits from publicizing moral infractions. Indeed, judging by the reporting on the presidential campaign, it seems that in the absence of any substantive public debate on morality among religious leaders, media representatives have emerged as the new priesthood in our culture: they demand confessions of misconduct from public figures and then determine the seriousness of the sin and the degree of penance required for the sin to be forgiven.

Claremont philosophy professor John Roth suggested that one way of restoring moral and ethical dialogue to public discourse would be to speak in a poetic or lyrical mode—close to what Fishburn described as an expressive mode. But as Fishburn and her committee discovered, the secular media make it virtually impossible to use that mode of expression.

Still, the task must be undertaken. As Robert Sollard wrote recently in the *Chronicle of Higher Education* (as cited by Roth), "Much has been written about the loss of ethics, a sense of decency, moderation and fair play in American society. I would submit that much of the loss is a result of increasing ignorance, in circles of presumably educated people, of religious and spiritual worldviews. It is difficult to imagine, for example, how ethical issues can be intelligently appreciated and discussed or how wise and thoughtful decisions can be reached without either knowledge or reference to these religious or spiritual principles that underlie our legal system and moral codes."

An ethical system requires a living tradition for constant revision and sustenance; cut off from that source, the system loses its force. Which is why we must find a way to engage in public discourse that will reflect the "religious or spiritual principles that underlie our legal system and moral codes."

We are left with an increasingly frustrating dilemma: a nation with the soul of a church has lost its way, but its traditional manner of speaking of ethics and values is considered politically incorrect. We must search for a language with which to address this predicament, without giving undue preference to any segment of our pluralistic culture. It is a problem with no easy solution.

THINKING IN PUBLIC

Where is Walter Lippmann when we really need him? That sort of public intellectual is a vanishing figure in our media-hyped culture. Thoughtful analysis of public issues for a wide audience, once the assignment of people like Lippmann, has virtually disappeared. In its place we have shouting matches on talk shows. William Dean, a professor at Gustavus Adolphus College, told a meeting of academics in Indianapolis recently that they were partly responsible for the decline in public intellectual life. In terms that rankled many in the audience, Dean argued that today's academy is so obsessed with the intellectual discussion within its halls that it fails to address issues of wider concern. Religious intellectuals must bear special blame for this abdication, Dean said.

Dean follows John Dewey in thinking that religion "is meant to unify the whole self in a totality with the universe." Accordingly, the religious community has a mandate to produce a thoughtful analysis of culture. But, he added, religious intellectuals shun those outside the academy, evidence a "professional preoccupation with credentials," and put their energy into debating issues within their special disciplines.

Speaking at a conference on "Public Expressions of Religion in America" sponsored by the Center for the Study of Religion and American Culture in Indianapolis, Dean suggested that the nonprofit organizations—specifically the nonacademic elements of the nonprofit sector—are the places where nuance and depth in public debate are being kept alive.

One can think of exceptions to Dean's rule. People like Garry Wills and Martin Marty are religious intellectuals who from their posts in the academy address the general public on large issues. On the other hand, many well-known religious intellectuals who speak to a wide audience—people like Richard Neuhaus or Michael Novak—are connected not to universities but to foundations.

Dean's jeremiad echoes a much earlier warning from political scientist Harold Lasswell about "disciplinary narrowness." This feature of academic life offers society an inadequate preparation for the future. Lasswell, who taught at both the University of Chicago and Yale before his death in 1978, made his appeal for interdisciplinary research in his 1956 presidential address to the American Political Science Association. In the mid-1960s Lasswell told a gathering at Purdue University that the task of the academy was to "case the joint"—a nonacademic phrase drawn from detective novels which suggests the need to look in every corner of the room for clues or hidden danger.

Public dialogue has disintegrated even further since Lasswell called on the academy to contribute to an understanding of society as a whole. Now, as Dean puts it, the academy is so professionalized that it has nothing to say to our common culture. This, says Dean, is one reason why "our culture is coming apart."

Robert Reich, the Harvard economist [who later served as secretary of labor in President Clinton's first term], reminds us in *The Resurgent Liberal* that public policy in this country is shaped by three currents of thought that have prevailed since the Enlightenment—bureaucratic expertise, democratic deliberation and utilitarianism. This means reliance on experts "uniquely skilled in using organization to accomplish complex tasks efficiently," a belief in the importance of public "conversation," and the grim realization that public interest is "an accommodation or aggregation of individual interests." Missing from this mixture, Reich argues, is any overarching value on which we might base "the inherent legitimacy of the policy decisions that result."

Reich would have policy-makers and policy-analysts discover ways "to engage the public in an ongoing dialogue over what problems should be addressed, what is at stake in such decisions, and how to strengthen the public's capacities to deal with similar problems in the future." Such a process, says Reich, would enable society to define and evaluate its collective goals and examine its beliefs and thus become "better able to mobilize its resources and achieve its goals."

As one looks over the presidential campaign of 1992, it is obvious that the closest we have come to examining our national norms and beliefs was the near-hysterical response by liberals to Dan Quayle's passing reference to Murphy Brown as an improper role model for young women, and the dark hints of theocracy that the religion-fearing media found in the Republican convention.

Reflecting on norms and ideals is the special province of the intellectual community, and it is the special responsibility of religious intellectuals. But if we accept Dean's analysis, religious scholars are just as preoccupied with their professional credentials as are their secular peers.

Looking to Dewey as his model, Dean would have us reach for values that "connect to the whole, new harmonies to resolve social discord." This was Dewey's way of speaking of ultimate concerns. In Dean's view, however, the academy's cautious stance has rendered it incapable of such a task. The task has been taken up by the nonprofit foundations and agencies that are envisioning solutions to social problems.

Dean may be too pessimistic about the academy and too hopeful about the nonprofit sector. But his broadside certainly got the attention of his audience, and the book he is developing on the same theme will likely provoke lively discussion. In light of the presidential campaign, when so many political participants and observers have been busy exploiting fear and anger and few have tried to "case the joint," it's a persuasive argument.

BLENDING COMMITMENT AND POLITICS

The notion that politicians must not permit their religious sensibilities to affect political decision-making has reduced political dialogue to a seminar on pragmatism. Political leaders might benefit from reflecting on a distinction Max Weber made between the morality of saints and the morality of politicians. In his classic essay "Politics as Vocation," Weber did not seek to remove ethics from politics but urged politicians to blend ethical commitment with a pragmatic ethic of responsibility.

In our highly secularized environment, politicians are intimidated from expressing a commitment to ethical standards. At best they fall back instead on safe phrases like "family values." Afraid of being branded as moralists, or even worse, proselytizers, politicians cling to surface arguments that remain in the public's comfort zone, choosing sides in the familiar debates on school prayer, pornography, media immorality and abortion.

Without an ethic of commitment behind our ethic of pragmatic responsibility there is no guide to being responsible. We have elevated pragmatism to the sole measurement of our political behavior. What moral discourse there is occurs in easily digestible sound bites: Murphy Brown sets a bad example; adoption is better than abortion; and (one of my favorites from Pat Buchanan) school prayer makes students productive.

Václav Havel, an author and the president of Czechoslovakia, argues in *Summer Meditations* (Knopf) that "all genuine politics" has a moral origin. Ralf Dahrendorf, writing in the *New York Times*, reflects on Weber's notion of politics and comments that "Havel's every page breathes the spirit that made him the authentic spokesman of the Eastern European revolution of 1989, which was in his words about 'living in truth.'" What is paramount to Havel the writer and what he now seeks to implement as a political leader is the belief that what finally matters is not power but "decency, reason, responsibility, sincerity, civility and tolerance."

Our attention, however, is focused almost entirely on solving short-term problems. Alice Hoffman's novel *Turtle Moon* has a character named Lucy, a young divorced mother distressed over the behavior of her teen-age son. Reflecting on the physical complaints she hears from other mothers about their children, she thinks, "There is, after all, strong brown soap for poison ivy, iodine for cuts and bruises, mud for bee stings, honey for sore throats, chalky white casts for broken bones. But where is the cure for meanness of spirit? What remedy is available for unhappiness and thievery? Certainly, if it were anywhere in Florida, Lucy would have found it, since the sharp yellow afternoon sunlight hides nothing. It's the sort of light that makes it difficult to begin all over again and doesn't allow for much invention. You are what you see in the mirror above the sink—in Lucy's case, a pretty woman with slightly green hair whose son hates her."

It is very difficult for our society to acknowledge the reality of "meanness of spirit," for there is no immediate cure for such a fundamental flaw. We do not solve the problems of urban decay by the application of brown soap or iodine. There is something seriously wrong with our society, but we do not begin to identify it. We have allowed the triumph of secularity to lull us into believing that meanness of spirit can be cured by a few Band-Aids, or ballistic missiles, or junk bonds.

To fill the vacuum left by the departure of religion from our public realm, with its diminution of spiritual goals, ideals and priorities, we have adopted a language that is ethically neutral. That neutrality leads us to elevate secularity to supremacy. The question that excites us is not, What is good? or What is just? or What is best for the larger community? but, Where's mine? The Los Angeles looters were first cousins of the Wall Street pirates who loot our corporations with their buyouts, or the CEOs who demand and receive salaries and bonuses equal to the budgets of some countries.

Having lost a sense of transcendence in our common life, we look for meaning in power, achievement and success. As a nation we have no basis of measurement by which to judge what is of value. A cover story in *Newsweek* inspired by the Murphy Brown discussion asked, "Whose values?" The question is proper; but the answer from *Newsweek* was remarkably obtuse. Accustomed as I am to seeing religion blanked out in secular discussions, I was still surprised to find that *Newsweek*'s various writers on the topic managed to ignore religion. One interview referred to the Baptist background of a woman who discussed how she raised her four sons. The interview itself, however, allowed for no reference to such basics as, say, the Ten Commandments, or sacrificial love, or loving one's neighbor as oneself.

One headline, "The Original Sin," suggested that here at last the topic might be examined within a religious framework. But alas, the reference was not to Eve, Adam or the fruit of the tree, but to a John F. Kennedy speech calling for deficit spending to jump-start the economy, a step the writer believes started us down the road to economic ruin. The "original sin" of the title referred to a sin against the one god in our culture that really matters.

Religious language is enough a part of our history that the magazine could play with the term "original sin" in the headline. Meanwhile, while media and political leaders carefully avoid religious references, a majority of Americans are expressing their frustration and anger either by not voting or by embracing candidates who promise quick and easy solutions to complex problems. It is time we said to our leaders that while we don't expect to elect any saints to public office, we have had more than enough of political pragmatism rooted in nothing but the desire to win the next election.

ABSOLUTES AND AMBIGUITIES

Ronald Reagan's 1980 transition to the White House has been viewed as a model of how a new president should shape his leadership team. Reagan had the advantage of a clear ideology. He did not need a long time to find his appointees, for they were all waiting patiently in the far right corner of the political spectrum. It won't be that easy for Bill Clinton, who ran a campaign that stayed cautiously in the broad political middle. The president-elect wants to shape an administration that "reflects America." An important way in which Clinton himself seems to reflect America is his religious sensibility. In a *New Republic* article published just before the election, Fred Barnes predicted that the influence of religion would be second only to the economy in shaping voter opinion. Virtually no other media analyst picked up on this insight. Barnes, who is an evangelical, quotes Catholic theologian and Bush-supporter George Wiegel as saying that Clinton "does not give off that aura of cold rational secularism that Dukakis did. He's not religiously tone deaf."

If it is true, as Barnes suggested, that Clinton's familiarity with the world of religion helped him win the election, we may nevertheless assume that his supporters wanted a leader who is also aware of the moral ambiguities of political decision-making. Absolutist moral positions will not resolve such complex problems as gays in the military, funding for AIDS research, disposition of nuclear waste, reduction of defense spending, or getting food to starving populations.

It is no judgment on George Bush's personal morality or spiritual nature to suggest that he simply did not know how to speak to the American public in the language of spiritual commitment. When he tried, he seemed to be reading from an ideological playbook handed him by Jerry Falwell.

During his 1988 campaign for the presidency, Bush talked about his experience of floating in the Pacific Ocean after his plane was shot down. Since he was looking back almost 50 years, we should not hold him to absolute accuracy about his thoughts on that occasion. But what he said is revealing: "I was floating around in a little yellow raft, setting a record for paddling. I thought of my family, my mom and dad, and the strength I got from them. I thought of my faith, the separation of church and state" (quoted in Bushisms, compiled by the editors of the *New Republic*).

Few Americans, and probably not Bush himself, believe that he was thinking at that moment about Madison, Jefferson and the glories of the First Amendment. Like most Americans of his generation and religious tradition, Bush is not comfortable speaking in public about his religious faith. The fault is not his alone; it lies more in the nature of his particular religious tradition and in the secularity of the societal elite that he knew would be judging what he was saying. By confining religion to the private sphere, or limiting it, in David Tracy's marvelous metaphor, to a "sacred reservation," our governing elite truncates or ignores an important dimension of American life. Bush has never been comfortable with religious language in public—though this has not stopped him from embracing the absolutist positions of some fundamentalists and some Catholics.

Early in his career Bush discovered that the best moral issues to take into the public arena are those that avoid ambiguity and appeal directly to strong surface emotions. In recent elections this approach has settled on the topics of abortion, homosexuality, pornography and prayer in school. For the 1992 election, it all came down to a neat package labeled "family values."

Absolutist positions are easily translated into presidential decrees or proposals for a constitutional amendment. The use of fetal tissue in medical research, for example, was banned by President Reagan in response to demands from pro-life groups. This is one of the presidential decrees that Clinton is expected to reverse, not because he "favors" abortions, but because he values research and does not believe that lifting the ban would set off a rash of abortions.

A religious sensibility rooted in a belief in forgiveness, grace and redemption sees life not as an arena of absolutism, but as one in which all our choices are less than they should be—but more than they would be without the grace of a redemptive, loving God. Approaching complex moral problems with an awareness of ambiguity can lead to solutions that are not locked into the ideology of the right or left.

At the University of Notre Dame, Clinton gave what one of his campaign aides described as a "defining speech." According to Barnes, it revealed the candidate as "an unabashed Christian and a man of strong religious sensibility." Barnes also pointed out that when Clinton appeared on VISN, an ecumenical cable network, he spoke with ease of his faith, which "enabled me to keep living and keep going and keep doing things." On the *MacNeil/Lehrer News Hour* Clinton spoke of how, "like other people, I have had crises in my life, personal crises, personal failures, the sense that I had let myself and others down, the sense that maybe I'd never be the person God wanted me to be."

In this confessional mode, Clinton used language that comes naturally to a person with his evangelical background. To contrast Clinton's comfort level with religious language with that of Bush is not to say that Clinton is a man of deeper moral conviction, but it does indicate that Clinton can relate more effectively to a public that is more "religious" than ideological in its public and private convictions.

Referring at Notre Dame to "the values behind" his "vision of America," Clinton said, "my faith is a source of pride to me, but far, far more important, it is a source of humility, because it teaches that none of us is a stranger to sin and weakness. It is a source of hope because it teaches that each of us is capable of redemption. And it is a source of challenge because it teaches that we must all strive to live according to our beliefs."

What can these beliefs offer us? They cannot offer us absolute moral answers to political questions. But they can point us toward a set of absolutes on which there is no disagreement in either secular or religious circles: honesty, service to community, responsibility, respect for others. As Kathleen Kennedy Townsend notes in an article on values in public schools, such ideals "have sufficiently universal appeal to serve as the founding and guiding principles of this country" ("Why Johnny Can't Tell Right from Wrong," *Washington Monthly*).

Townsend, director of the Maryland Student Service Alliance for the Maryland Department of Education [and now lieutenant governor of Maryland], calls on schools to begin paying attention to the ways they can, even in a pluralistic society, transmit moral values. And according to Townsend, the impact is striking: "A survey of 176 schools that have adopted a values curriculum found that 77 percent report a decrease in discipline problems, 68 percent boasted an increase in attendance, and 64 percent showed a decrease in vandalism." So why aren't we teaching values in public schools? Because, Townsend suggests, "there has been no political or popular consensus that values should be as much a part of the curriculum as reading and writing."

Perhaps Clinton, guided by his Southern Baptist faith, is in a position to shape the "political and popular consensus" on the necessity—in teaching and in politics—of honesty, service, responsibility and respect for others. After all, if an anticommunist named Richard Nixon could be the one to open up relations with communist China, then maybe a child of the '60s, the era that challenged traditional values, can be the one to call us to a consensus on values.

At Notre Dame Clinton alluded to a fundamental biblical theme when he said, "To the terrible question of Cain—am I my brother's (and sister's) keeper?—the only possible answer for us is a thunderous yes." The months ahead will show us how much Clinton's administration can link its problem-solving agenda to the imperatives of that "thunderous yes."

A SEARCH FOR MEANING

With its usual cynicism, the *New Republic* offered to help "those still mystified by Hillary Rodham Clinton's spiritual quest," which surfaced recently in a talk she gave in Austin, Texas, on "the politics of meaning." To resolve the public's presumed mystification, *TNR* reprinted a section of the Austin talk alongside a snippet from a speech she gave as a college senior in 1969. There is an understandable consistency between the two sets of comments. But *TNR*, which is emerging as the *Osservatore Romano* of our national secular faith, used this consistency to ridicule Clinton as someone who has not left her youthful confusions behind.

The Hillary of 1969 was a harmless Wellesley student, but the Hillary of 1993 is a powerful political figure in the White House. She and her husband have not been pleasing to *TNR* because they have veered away from being New Democrats toward being oldline liberals. And the secular thought police are warning her to keep her Sunday school piety to herself, or else she will suffer the same fate as that other moralist, Jimmy Carter, who tried to explain his motives in language that resonated with his spiritual tradition. Ironically, two of *TNR*'s better-known writers, Fred Barnes and Morton Kondracke, make no secret of their religious sensibilities, even writing about their faith on occasion. But they never make the "mistake" of justifying political analysis in religious terms.

If Hillary Clinton is to play a serious leadership role, she has to be true to herself, and that involves faithfulness to her religious story. That's what she was exhibiting when she asked her audience at the University of Texas, "Why is it in a country as wealthy as we are . . . there is this undercurrent of discontent, this sense that somehow economic growth and prosperity, political democracy and freedom are not enough, that we lack meaning in our individual lives and meaning collectively—this sense that our lives are part of some greater effort, that we are connected to one another?"

Unfortunately, Clinton did not go far enough. For the large public which does relate to religious language, she sounded too secular; there was little in her speech that reflected her personal faith. And for the protectors of secularism, she sounded too spiritual.

In a *New York Times Magazine* article on her religious background, Clinton acknowledged that she got the term "politics of meaning" from Michael Lerner, editor and publisher of the liberal Jewish magazine *Tikkun*. In Austin she defined the "politics of meaning" as a "new ethos of individual responsibility and caring."

Chicago Tribune columnist Clarence Page made light of this quest by suggesting that she was repeating a pattern from her youth. "In the '60s . . . it was fashionable to wrestle with the world's problems . . . over Turkish rugs and under psychedelic posters." Page suggested her search was typical of her generation. Like other baby boomers, she had been influenced by a variety of figures: "At various times [she was] under the sway of Barry Goldwater, Martin Luther King Jr., Saul Alinsky, Paul Tillich, John Wesley, John Lindsay, Eugene McCarthy, Nelson Rockefeller and Marian Wright Edelman, to name a few."

Page gleaned his list from interviews with Clinton. To his credit, he included John Wesley, a name that many readers outside of Methodism—the tradition to which Hillary Clinton continues to belong—might not know.

Page was not as cynical in linking Clinton to the '60s as was the *New Republic*, but he made essentially the same point when he counseled the Clintons to articulate a "clear vision of where they want Americans to go, then take us there." And that is good advice. The image of incompetence ($200 haircuts, nannygate and travelgate) has begun to creep into public perceptions of the Clinton White House and undermine the president's ability to sell his programs to the public and to Congress. Still, it is early in this administration. The Clintons have time to implement their political program and to articulate a spiritual tone of leadership.

Americans have deep religious traditions, and they are far more religious than political, academic and media leaders acknowledge. These leaders—and Dan Quayle was right in calling them a "cultural elite"—are so committed to a secular interpretation of reality that they will devote considerable energy to debunking the sort of spiritual quest that surfaced in Clinton's Austin speech. It may be easier to convince Congress to pass an economic package than it is to communicate a "politics of meaning" through secular media. Secularists can be as obdurate in their beliefs as religious folk.

Page cited Paul Tillich as one of the influences on Hillary Clinton's spiritual journey, and Tillich indeed represents a good place to begin. As John P. Newport has written, Tillich defined his theological task as that of helping to lead "the cultured among the despisers" of religion to rediscover the "lost dimension of cultural life which is the religious dimension." In her search for a "politics of meaning," Hillary Clinton might well follow Tillich's method of correlation—connecting the questions that naturally arise in human experience to theological concerns. This was how Tillich sought, in Newport's phrase, to be "in conversation with humanistically educated skeptics."

Newport, whose book on Tillich in the "Makers of the Modern Theological Mind" series has been reissued in a hardback edition by Hendrickson Press, told me that he recently revised his thinking on Tillich somewhat to put greater emphasis on the personal and prophetic dimensions of the faith. But he agrees that Tillich's dialogue with intellectuals on questions of "ultimate concern" remains a valid way to approach today's "cultured despisers" of religion.

Hillary Clinton and her husband might take a look at Tillich or Newport on Tillich. And they might also be interested in *The Search for Meaning* (Abingdon), a book by Magdalena Naylor, Thomas Naylor and William Willimon that grew out of a seminar at Duke University. The authors cite as inspiration for the seminar a poll conducted at Duke's Fuqua School of Business in which the vast majority of students responded to a question about what they wanted from school by declaring: "Money, power and things." Such goals leave students hungry for meaning.

A future Clinton speech might well make use of this quote from Elie Wiesel, cited in *The Search for Meaning*: "When Adam first opened his eyes he asked God, 'Who am I?' rather than 'Who are you?'" A quest for meaning or, for that matter, for health care reform cannot be conducted without some reference to an ultimate concern.

Hillary Rodham Clinton is not trying to convert secularists to her particular brand of religion. In her quest for the "politics of meaning," she seeks only to touch the spiritual roots of this nation. She should continue to make her case.

GOD AS A HOBBY

Bill Clinton has been touting a new book, *The Culture of Disbelief*, by Stephen Carter, who argues that our culture rejects religion as a valid source for public discourse. Carter had considered as a title for his book a phrase he uses as a chapter heading, "God as a hobby," a reference to the view that belief in God is acceptable only if it remains a private and personal enterprise, like collecting stamps or model trains. In addressing the same topic, theologian David Tracy has used the metaphor of a "sacred reservation," where, it is understood, religion is to be confined for private consideration.

When the media learned that Clinton was praising Carter's book (he urged a group of religious leaders at a White House breakfast to go out and buy it) Carter immediately became the center of considerable attention. He was interviewed by Charleyne Hunter Gault on the *McNeil-Lehrer News Hour*, and drew the ire of columnist Michael Kinsley, who attacked Carter in the *New Republic* and again on a CNN panel program.

Kinsley says it is obvious that Carter is wrong about our culture. Evidence: it would be political suicide for any politician to announce that he or she is a nonbeliever. ("Hi, my name is John, I am an atheist and I want to be your governor.") Since no politician would take the atheist pledge it must follow that we live in a believing society that demands religious commitment of its leaders.

But Kinsley's argument hardly refutes Carter. Indeed, the fact that people expect a religious profession in a politician illustrates in a way Carter's central thesis—religious faith is regarded as part of an acceptable personal package (happy wife, smiling children) but is not significantly related to public discourse.

Carter contends that "we have created a political and legal culture that presses the religiously faithful to be other than themselves, to act publicly, and sometimes privately as well, as though their faith does not matter to them." John F. Kennedy gave a classic articulation of this bifurcation when he assured Baptist ministers in Texas that his religious faith would not influence his political decisions. He would be, as the old joke puts it, "not religious enough to count."

In her interview with Carter, Hunter Gault seemed unaware of Carter's contention that, for believers, religion is the driving force of behavior. She was worried about minority religious beliefs being imposed on the majority, which Carter had described as the fear of "any religious element in public moral discourse as a tool of the radical right for reshaping American society."

The influence of groups like the Christian Coalition on public life has only recently alerted the media to religion in public life. But secular indifference and, in some cases, open hostility to the religious dimension in American culture was identified many years ago by William F. Buckley in *God and Man at Yale,* in which he wrote that the academy considered God-talk irrelevant. Writing with youthful indignation after completing his undergraduate work at Yale, Buckley found that God was not only banished but was an embarrassment to sophisticates.

At a recent conference on "Public Perceptions of the Press" at the University of Maryland, I felt obliged to say a few words for God. The dean of the journalism school had assumed I would make my usual case that secular media discount religion as a base from which to speak or act. Not wanting to disappoint him or God, I referred to a story several years ago in the *New York Times* that reported on a case in which a group of African-Americans had been sacrificing lambs as part of a religious ceremony. They were arrested and charged with some crime having to do with cruelty to animals. The *Times* story was obviously written from the perspective of the Society for the Prevention of Cruelty to Animals, a worthy secular organization which helps shape our thinking on nonhuman creatures. There was no indication that the *Times* reporter had any sympathy for the possibility that these believers had a religious rationale for killing the lambs. I thought it was a good example of media indifference to religious faith.

The journalism dean cornered me at dinner and said he was glad I had brought up my favorite topic. But did I have to start with animal sacrifice? Properly chastened, in a later session I spoke more specifically of the Christian faith as a motivating base for dialogue and action in society. It was not the media's failure to respect religion as an objective presence in society that concerned me, but rather the media's inability to comprehend how religious faith as a subjective reality—rooted, for the most part, in a believing community—could be the driving force in an individual's life.

One of the participants responded immediately and predictably: "Like Jim Bakker and Jimmy Swaggart?" Such linkage of clergy misconduct with religion has become as automatic as the connection between "damn" and "Yankees" was in the South of my childhood. The notion that religion is a matter for private consideration, and therefore inappropriate for public discourse, is so ingrained in American culture that when religion ventures off the reservation it is presumed to be intemperate or weird. (William Buckley says that it has been his experience that if a guest mentions God once at a dinner party the reference is greeted with silence; mention God twice, and there are no further invitations to dinner.)

The Culture of Disbelief is a valuable contribution to the discussion of religion and public life. The situation Carter describes is not new; modernity has been stepping on religion since the Enlightenment. As a Yale law professor, not one of those professional religious types who make their living being religious (or obnoxious), Carter is receiving a respectable hearing; he can't easily be dismissed, in the current popular phrase, as a "Waco wacko."

In their efforts to affect public policy, mainline religious liberals largely gave up on God-talk in public discourse, preferring the neutral language of their secular allies. Until recent decades this could be done honorably, since it was assumed that the prevailing mind-set of American culture was Protestant orthodoxy. But the reality and the awareness of pluralism destroyed that approach. And the tolerance and civility that are a priority for liberals soon led to a total retreat into secular language. Language, however, affects perspective. Keep quiet about God long enough, and succeeding generations will assume that out of sight and speech is out of mind.

Kinsley is correct to say that a public declaration of unbelief is politically incorrect. He is wrong, however, to think this indicates that ours is a culture of faith. Ours is a culture of disbelief—and it is so in large measure because that is the way we want it to be. It is politically correct to claim a religious cover, but politically incorrect to testify that we are acting on our religious claims. Could it be that those operating with respectable religious fronts are as reluctant as nonbelievers to use or hear God-talk in public discourse because they have never really internalized their faith?

We live in a culture of disbelief not because the media or nonbelievers want it that way, but because those who claim to be religious are afraid someone will say they sound "like Bakker and Swaggart." Who wants to be known as someone who listens to an unseen power? That's weird.

LANGUAGE GAP

A group of journalists and religious leaders met recently in Evanston, Illinois, to consider how to organize a new Media and Religion Center linking a theological seminary (Garrett-Evangelical) and a journalism school (Northwestern's). One of the participants, *New York Times* religion writer Peter Steinfels, observed that one challenge of such a project is overcoming the lack of a common language. For the news media, said Steinfels, "popular fiction provides a reference point that was once provided to an earlier public by Shakespeare or the Bible." An allusion to the television character Murphy Brown is instantly recognized by the public as a reference to a single parent. People who no longer resonate to stories about prodigal sons or unfaithful servants are familiar with lines from popular movies ("Make my day," "We'll always have Paris"). Shakespeare may get better and more frequent film treatment than the Bible and is more readily taught in the public schools, but this rich resource of the English language is largely unknown to the general public. (I once shouted to a colleague at a Democratic National Convention, "Once more unto the breach, dear friends, once more!" and drew an uncomprehending stare.)

Few reporters at the site of the Branch Davidian disaster at

Waco, Texas, were prepared to interpret David Koresh's use of the Bible. According to one of the Evanston participants, one reporter, when informed that Koresh was relying on the Book of Revelation, asked, "Where do you find that book?" (A theologian present insisted that he had heard a reporter ask, in another context, how to spell "Jesus.")

Participants at the Evanston gathering were in general agreement that the media are so thoroughly secular that even when they want to talk about religion they are easily led astray. There is something slightly off-kilter, for example, in the way in which some Christians are able to persuade journalists that abortion is a scriptural abomination and that Jesus abhorred homosexuality, when in fact neither topic commands any serious biblical attention. The two issues have become central to the "religious" debate not because they are crucial to any single faith but because journalists have been persuaded that they are.

In other areas, journalists are less willing to accept others' definition of what is important. Science or education reporters know their subjects well enough to set their own agenda and to determine the significance of the newest fad. There are superb religion reporters at work today—including Steinfels, John Dart of the *Los Angeles Times* and Richard Ostling of *Time*—but often covering the religion beat is but one remove from working on the obituary page in print journalism's pecking order. (The recent addition of a religion reporter at ABC News—the first at a major television outlet—only underscores how little attention nonprint journalists pay to the topic.)

The absence of a language shared by religion and journalism is a problem that has its counterpart in government. This is apparent in a hot new political book, Bob Woodward's *The Agenda: Inside the Clinton White House*. The work has to be taken with a touch of salt, since Woodward's sources (usually unnamed) have their own agenda to promote. But Woodward's narrative does suggest that the war raging within the administration for the soul of Bill Clinton is a struggle between the president's elite intellectual friends and the media consultants who want to retain the themes that were pushed in his campaign.

Woodward writes of the initial motivation with which Clinton's media team fashioned his campaign, and he reports on an impassioned speech Hillary Clinton gave at a Camp David meeting of advisers: "'You show people what you're willing to fight for when you fight your friends,' Hillary said." (She was recalling the struggle she and her husband had with teachers over school reform in Arkansas.) She noted how her husband used that wonderful quote from Isaiah, "Where there is no vision, the people perish," in his convention acceptance speech. "The vision, she said, was in a sense the plan for the journey ahead. They could not get bogged down in bond market talk and deficit reduction numbers. Those were just tools. They were not the vision; they were not the journey."

Woodward concludes that in spite of Hillary's passion and Clinton's longing to maintain his campaign themes, the harsh realities of the political process have led him to step away from the issues—such as job development—on which he was elected. At one point in a preinaugural meeting, Woodward says, after viewing elaborate charts and listening to his economic advisers tell him he had to make decisions that would placate the financial community, "Clinton's face turned red with anger and disbelief. 'You mean to tell me that the success of the program and my re-election hinges on the Federal Reserve and a bunch of [deleted] bond traders?'"

In his many interviews Woodward failed to pick up any indication of the importance of religious faith in the Clinton White House. He may not have noticed it because the struggle there has more to do with a method of communication than with policies. The Clintons seem reluctant to use spiritual language to make the case urged on them by their advisers. It is possible to speak of sacrifice, commitment, responsibility and the common good in a way Americans can understand and respond to. (Check out Abraham Lincoln's Civil War speeches.) But the Clintons have difficulty doing so, and the secular media are no help.

Theologian Anne E. Carr says in her book on Thomas Merton that Merton's religious writing "functions through image and symbol rather than through logic and argument in suggesting more than it literally says, in connoting both the familiar and the unknown, both present experience and future possibility. It is a language that speaks to the heart as well as the head." Bill Clinton knows the language of the heart. He used it effectively in his campaign. Though the secular media won't make it easy, he needs to use that language in shaping and selling his policies.

PASSION IN PUBLIC

Patrick Anderson wrote speeches for Jimmy Carter during the 1976 campaign for president. He took the assignment because it was a "new adventure" in writing. After Carter's inauguration, Anderson, who had earlier written one novel, *The President's Mistress*, decided to turn his campaign notes into a book. But since his wife was working at the White House it seemed unwise to go public with his thoughts, so he put aside the memoir and forgot about it. Almost two decades later, Anderson's account, with some updating, has been published as *Electing Jimmy Carter: The Campaign of 1976* (Louisiana State University Press).

The book is fascinating because of the way Anderson is both drawn to one side of Carter—his idealism and his "interesting mind—open, curious and creative"—and repelled by another—the side that led to frequent lapses into "Sunday-school homilies." Electing Jimmy Carter tells us more about Anderson's antireligious feeling than it does about Carter. The candor of the book and the fact that it was written almost two decades ago make it a milestone in the continuing attempt to fathom what really motivates Jimmy Carter.

Anderson confesses that he did not understand Carter because the side of the president that struggled with sin and pride never made any sense to him. To Anderson, Carter the preacher overwhelmed Carter the politician. There was no second term because "his endless, ill-concealed, eye-popping sanctimony became insufferable; it was not so much the economy or the hostage crisis that cost him the 1980 election, I thought, as it was his maddening piety."

Anderson's book is a meanspirited but revealing reminder of how Carter's public image was shaped by his enemies. In the breathless, novelistic style of a book written on the run during the campaign, the author admits his disdain for Carter's religious perspective and style.

Anderson provides, unwittingly, an example of the person who continues to be irritated by a man who builds houses for the poor, searches for cures for exotic African diseases, plunges into the problems of urban slums in Atlanta, and still finds time to talk dictators out of going to war.

What would motivate someone to spend so much time doing good? Anderson can find no answer, because he is looking in the wrong places. Anderson is tone deaf to religion. He is puzzled over Carter's obsessive desire to avoid the sin of pride. Why can't he be like the rest of us and admit he wants to succeed? Why does he need to worry about human motivation in the first place? *Electing Jimmy Carter* is evidence of how some people get angry at Carter's insistence on doing good when he could be doing well.

After Carter helped broker the agreement that paved the way for the removal of Haiti's military dictators and the return of Jean-Bertrand Aristide to the presidency, one editorial cartoon showed Carter standing in front of the White House and holding a sign saying, "Will work for the Nobel Peace Prize." Since his critics cannot believe that anyone would do good for the sake of doing good, there must be some other explanation for what keeps Carter on the road or on the phone talking with world leaders, trying to solve problems.

Anderson offers this analysis of the motives of former presidents: "Our ex-presidents tend to get what they want. Nixon wanted to be rehabilitated. Ford wanted to play golf and make money. Bush wanted to be a Texan. Carter, a more complex man, wants . . . what? To be respected? To be loved? To have us say we were wrong? A Nobel Peace Prize?"

For Anderson, Carter's religious faith is his fatal flaw, the dark side that prevented him from a successful presidency. Carter was "enslaved by a guilt-ridden, sin-saturated theology that told him that half the country was wallowing in the devil's embrace." The *Playboy* interview in which Carter spoke of his biblical understanding of lust is described by Anderson as the first major sign that Carter was out of step with the American people. "Pressed about the 'sins' of adultery and homosexuality, [Carter] declared that you can't legislate morality, but later he added, defensively, plaintively, that these were sins and 'I can't change the teachings of Christ.'" Anderson concludes: "It must have been an awful burden, all his own imagined sins and the world's too. But he couldn't change the Bible or change himself, and in time he lost us."

Regarding religion as a dark burden that enlightened people

ought to outgrow, Anderson misinterprets Carter's words and actions. He cannot comprehend how religion is part burden, yes, but also solace and inspiration.

In a recent issue of *Media/Critic*, Fred Barnes of the *New Republic* recalled a 1985 discussion that a group of journalists had with Governor Mario Cuomo of New York. The talk followed dinner at an Italian restaurant, so it was more of a friendly exchange than a press conference. At one point Cuomo explained why he had sent his children to Catholic schools. "Children are taught that it is a God-centered universe at parochial schools," Barnes recalled Cuomo saying. "At public schools, God is not mentioned in the classroom."

The governor added that he did not expect public schools to teach about God. But a blackout on God in the schools "affects kids." And, he added, "the public schools inculcate a disbelief in God. They make a child wonder, 'If God's so important how come they never mention Him?'" Barnes was sympathetic to Cuomo's concern, but "from the reaction of my colleagues, one might have thought Cuomo had advocated mandatory snake-handling as a test of faith for the state's students. The journalists showered him with dozens of unfriendly questions." (Anderson recalls that during a campaign stop at the San Diego zoo, Carter's aides went into a frenzy when the candidate picked up a huge snake: they feared that photos of Carter and the snake would evoke the snake-handling image.)

One columnist who attended the Cuomo dinner wrote in the *New York Daily News*: "There is something disturbing about the suggestion that the governor of the state of New York regards that state's public education as spiritually blighted." While Cuomo would not try to "impose his religious views on others," the columnist acknowledged, there are those who might "take the logical and necessary next step" and push to require organized prayer in schools.

This reaction is replicated in critics who don't want to appear intolerant but who display "I get nervous" signals, suggesting that any public expression of religious belief will inevitably lead to unacceptable forms of religious politics. A story in the *New York Times Magazine* on the Religious Right quotes moderate Republican candidate Bobbie Kilberg after she was defeated in a Virginia campaign by a Christian Right candidate: "It is positive to have people of faith—all faiths—participating in the political process and running for office, but I get very nervous when I am told that only Christians, preferably those who are 'born again,' should be elected, that evolution should not be taught in the public schools, and that I am not a Republican if I am pro-choice. I get even more nervous when people tell me that they have been directed by God to support a candidate and that the right to arm yourself with assault weapons is necessary to protect a 'Christian nation' against the heathen onslaught."

I am shocked, shocked I say, to hear that people can be passionate about politics. I vividly recall the passions that fueled delegates to the 1972 Democratic National Convention, at which George McGovern was nominated and antiwar activists denounced Richard Nixon for not ending the immoral conflict in Vietnam.

We may not like the political conclusions reached by the Christian Right, and we may disagree with the object of its passions. But different tactics and faulty conclusions are part of the democratic process. What is not a part of that process is the belief that the only passion off limits for public discourse is that which is rooted in religious faith. Fortunately, Jimmy Carter doesn't share that belief.

GIVE ALL YOU CAN

Tired of all this talk about orphanages, Newt Gingrich's book deal and the speaker's views on the First Lady? Of course. So let's turn to the sermons of John Wesley. The fact that the founder of the Methodist movement recently attracted the attention of the speaker of the house is far more important than anything Kathleen Gingrich might whisper to Connie Chung. Gingrich's inaugural address to the House of Representatives included a ringing call for a "Wesleyan revival." He wants Americans to be morally reinvigorated and to devote more time and money to help the poor. *Newsweek* columnist Joe Klein suggested that Gingrich could bolster his message with references to a new book by Gertrude Himmelfarb, *The De-Moralization of Society,* which argues that "Victorian attitudes toward charity—and poverty—were not only admirable but quite successful." An even better resource, however, would be John Wesley, whose evangelistic zeal and social commitment are credited with helping the British avoid the civil upheaval that led to the French Revolution.

Many Americans, aware that Republicans' antipathy toward government may mean the elimination of programs that help society's most vulnerable people, are leery of Gingrich's Contract with America. Klein complains that Gingrich is opposed even to Americorps, a program begun by President Clinton that promotes volunteer service. Patterned after the Peace Corps, Americorps recruits young people to work at nonprofit organizations for minimum wage while repaying college loans. Klein quotes Gingrich as saying he is "totally, unequivocally opposed to national service. It is coerced voluntarism . . . It's gimmickry." That sounds more like a political sound bite than the views of a man seeking a "Wesleyan revival."

But let's put Americorps aside. One general principle that Gingrich appears to endorse—the prudent use of money—may be found in Wesley's sermon "The Use of Money," based on the parable of the Rich Man and the Dishonest Steward (Luke 16). Wesley chose one of the more troubling of Jesus' parables—featuring what one writer terms "an arrant rascal" who cheats his master—to launch his exposition on how Christians should utilize money. By using a less than attractive example of managing money—the steward marks down bills owed to his master—Wesley made the point that while the love of money might be the root of all evil, the believer must be prudent in using money. *The Interpreter's Bible* comments: "Luke apparently believed that all money has some taint about it, and that the only redeeming feature of its possession is that it can be expended for righteous purposes."

This sermon contains Wesley's famous edict: "Gain all you can; save all you can; give all you can." Each of these points is surrounded by caveats. When speaking of the necessity to "gain all you can," Wesley says we must not harm our health or engage in work that would be unhealthy for "persons of a weak constitution." (Wesley warned against writing, which could be unhealthy for some since it requires many hours of sitting in an "uneasy posture"—an admonition the prolific author did not apply to himself.) Labor should not harm our own body and mind, nor that of our neighbor, nor should it involve the sale of "spirituous liquors" except for medicinal purposes.

As for saving, Wesley cautions against buying anything that isn't absolutely needed. He assails "superfluous or expensive apparel . . . needless ornaments . . . superfluous or expensive furniture . . . costly pictures, paintings, books . . . elegant (rather than useful) gardens." Savings, however, are not to be stashed away, buried "in the earth, as in your chest, or in the Bank of England." Money is meant to be used. "Having first gained all you can, and secondly saved all you can, then give all you can."

Wesley, in this sermon at least, does not call for tithing. No 10 percent for him: "'Render unto God,' not a tenth, nor a third, not half, but 'all that is God's.'" Wesley concludes with an emphatic call: "No more sloth! Whatsoever your hand findest to do, do it with your might. No more waste! Cut off every expense which fashion, caprice, or flesh and blood demands. No more covetousness! But employ whatever God has entrusted you with in doing good, all possible good, in every possible kind and degree, to the household of faith, to all men."

Those outside the circle of faith are not likely to respond to this sort of Wesleyan revivalism, as Gingrich must know. He is not speaking strictly of a religious revival. What he appears to be advocating, rather, is a sense of stewardship, which would include, at the outset, "three hours a month helping someone who needed it."

Robert L. Payton, of Indiana University's Center on Philanthropy, argues that Western civilization has always contained a mix of government assistance and personal giving to those in need. He points to Queen Elizabeth I's preamble to the Statute of Charitable Uses in 1601 as the beginning of the Poor Laws, through which government supported "poor people . . . sick and maimed soldiers and mariners . . . orphans . . . houses of corrections . . . the marriage of poor maids." Each society, says Payton, must ask how much aid should be expected from each of four sources: self-help; mutual aid (families and associations); government assistance; and voluntary philanthropy (large and small gifts and donations of time).

"What the 1994 congressional elections called for," observes Payton, "was a shift away from government support and a move toward more voluntary support, just as Lyndon Johnson's re-election in 1964 shifted the nation's policies toward increased government support."

The political shift does not appear to be accompanied, however, by a new willingness on the part of individuals to pick up a larger share of voluntary aid. A recent study by Independent Sector, a coalition of more than 800 voluntary organizations, foundations and corporate giving programs, found that the average household's donation to charity declined from $978 in 1989 to $880 in 1993. The study also noted a strong correlation between giving and voluntary service. "Those households with one or more volunteers gave an average of $1,193 [while] households that gave money but had no volunteers gave an average of $425."

While Gingrich is calling for three hours of volunteer service per month, the Independent Sector has a campaign called Give Five that asks citizens to give five hours of volunteer service per week and 5 percent of annual income to "the causes you care about." Giving five hours and 5 percent would double the current rate of giving, which averages two and one-half half hours per week and 2.5 percent of income.

Gingrich may not be expecting the religious community to assume the burden he wants the government to relinquish, but if there is to be a boom in giving and volunteering, it will likely come from religious groups. According to Payton, "Of all the money and time given to care for the needy today, at least half goes through organized religion, and according to another recent research finding, those people who attend church frequently (25 percent of the population) have a disproportionately large influence on all philanthropic giving and service."

Payton cited Ernest Gellner's recent book *Conditions of Liberty*, which contrasts economic attitudes in Wesley's 18th century with those of the 20th. When Wesley preached his sermon on the use of money, British society had a far greater sense of obligation toward the poor than does modern society. Though there was considerable disparity between rich and poor in 19th-century England, the sense of responsibility about using one's wealth was greater then than it is today.

Gingrich is on to something when he says that we need a Wesleyan-style revival leading to "moral reinvigoration" and a sense of civic responsibility. We are a long way from such a sense, however, and even further from the vision of mutual aid that John Calvin articulated in the *Institutes of the Christian Religion*: "Let this, therefore, be our rule for generosity and beneficence: We are the stewards of everything God has conferred on us by which we are able to help our neighbor, and are required to render account of our stewardship. Moreover, the only right stewardship is that which is tested by the rule of love."

Rather than being poised to assume a larger proportion of service to the needy, Americans appear to be headed in the opposite direction. The late Christopher Lasch, in his posthumously published book *The Revolt of the Elites and the Betrayal of Democracy*, laments "a lust for immediate gratification [that] pervades American society from top to bottom. There is a universal concern with the self—with 'self-fulfillment' and more recently with 'self-esteem,' slogans of a society incapable of generating a sense of civil obligation." Lasch's point seems confirmed by the sobering news that at the same time Americans are voting to cut government spending on the poor, they are cutting back on their own charitable giving and volunteering.

PRAYER TIME

When basketball star Mahmoud Abdul-Rauf of the Denver Nuggets came to Chicago recently to play against the Bulls, he planned to meet with 25 children in the area who suffer from Tourette's syndrome, a neurological disorder characterized by various motor and vocal tics. Abdul-Rauf himself suffers from Tourette's, and as an NBA standout he serves as a role model for children trying to cope with the malady. But the meeting with the kids was canceled. Abdul-Rauf was under intense media scrutiny and had to travel with security personnel that weekend, so it was difficult for him to move around the city.

Abdul-Rauf had been thrust into the national spotlight after the Denver media discovered that he was not standing for the singing of the national anthem. A devout Muslim, Abdul-Rauf had concluded that showing such respect for the U.S. flag was a violation of his religious beliefs. Once his refusal became known, the NBA suspended him, citing its rule requiring players to stand respectfully for the anthem.

The suspension was lifted when Abdul-Rauf decided that during the anthem he could stand and pray, his hands held in front of his face in the traditional Muslim manner. In his first game back after the suspension, Abdul-Rauf was roundly booed by Chicago fans. He managed to score 19 points in the Nuggets' loss.

Watching him sitting on the bench, with boos raining down on him because he had taken what he felt was a principled stand based on his religion, one could see the facial tics and head twists that characterize people with Tourette's. The syndrome has not interfered with Abdul-Rauf's basketball skills, however. He was a first-round draft pick (as a sophomore) out of Louisiana State University in 1990, and though small by NBA standards, he has been his team's playmaker and leading scorer. Raised as a Baptist under the name of Chris Jackson, Abdul-Rauf converted to Islam.

Talk radio hosts and sports writers blasted Abdul-Rauf for his refusal to stand, and then for his willingness to compromise. Of course, not all NBA players stand respectfully for the anthem. Some are rocking back and forth, others are joshing with their teammates. As for the spectators, many ignore the anthem altogether; they are busy getting to their seats or munching on hot dogs. At the Nuggets game, though, the Chicago crowd was very attentive, and their cheers displayed a record level of patriotism.

Abdul-Rauf's experience calls to mind another athlete's protest in the name of his religious commitment: Eric Liddell, later to serve as a Christian missionary to China, who was a member of Great Britain's track team at the 1924 Paris Olympics. As recounted in the 1981 movie *Chariots of Fire*, when Liddell discovered that in order to qualify for the 100-meter race he would have to run a heat on a Sunday, he refused to compete. Raised in the Scottish Congregational Church, Liddell believed that competing on the Sabbath would be a sin. The sports world was shocked, but Liddell did not change his mind. He eventually won a gold medal in the 400-meter race.

Chariots of Fire won a best-picture Academy Award, and audiences widely admired Liddell's stand on behalf of his faith. But Liddell was a Christian, and Abdul-Rauf is a Muslim. Might we draw some conclusions from this about the public's attitude toward Islam?

Consider also the recent movie *Executive Decision*, in which a courageous American foils an attempt to blow up a jetliner by a team of Islamic terrorists. Their leader is a mean, tough but quiet-mannered Muslim who reads from the Qur'an and sings the praises of Islam when he is not bullying the plane's passengers. For years "Arab terrorist" has been a handy movie villain. Perhaps now that category includes the fanatic, practicing Muslim.

There is much in Mahmoud Abdul-Rauf to admire. Besides being skilled at basketball, he is able to ignore the boos of rude fans and hold to his religious convictions. The television cameras usually ignore the singing of the national anthem, but for a time they will focus on Abdul-Rauf. Point him out to your children. Tell them that he is a Muslim, and that he is not a terrorist. Tell them that to play basketball with Tourette's syndrome is not an easy assignment. And explain that Abdul-Rauf took a stand based on his interpretation of his faith. Be sure to tell them about the boos and his scoring 19 points.

SPEAKING OF RELIGION

Biblical scholars have long debated the historical reliability of Matthew, Mark, Luke and John. Though there was not that much new to report on the topic, the three major newsmagazines decided anyway to feature Jesus on their Easter week cover and report on recent arguments about whether Jesus actually said what the New Testament says he said. Not surprisingly, the peg for the stories was the Jesus Seminar, which has been attracting media attention for some time. With their cover stories, *Time, Newsweek* and *U.S. News & World Report* were able simultaneously to acknowledge the belief of millions of Christians around the world while providing the "news" that the basis of Christian belief is something even Christian scholars disagree about.

No matter what millions of worshipers may celebrate on Easter Sunday, the resurrection of Jesus is still, in media parlance, an "alleged" event. The conflict between religion and scientific rationality is a phenomenon tailor-made for the news media, and it's the kind of conflict they are used to covering.

Media coverage of religion is not biased against religious faith; it is biased in favor of Enlightenment rationality. Our culture's embrace of scientific rationality as the ultimate measure of all reality has pushed religious faith over into a corner of irrelevancy. Even religion's most informed advocates are reluctant to speak of their faith in public settings for fear of rejection by their intellectual peers.

On a special Easter Sunday edition of *Meet the Press*, several prominent politicians were asked how they could justify being religious and political at the same time. Even former New York Governor Mario Cuomo, one of the most articulate Christian political leaders, seemed uncomfortable as he fielded questions from moderator Tim Russert that hinted there is something nefarious about religious groups receiving government funds for programs that serve the public. Russert repeatedly pressed his concern that public funds in church hands might expose recipients to the danger of conversion. Horrors. Russert should watch *Guys and Dolls*. A little preaching and a little soup rarely hurts, and it sometimes helps.

Before we leave the Sunday morning talk shows, we might ask why the networks present the programs geared for the more thoughtful segment of the audience during the traditional hours for Sunday worship. Do they assume the intellectual community is staying at home on Sunday morning? The ads for the Sunday morning programs make it clear the corporate sponsors believe that their image-building campaigns are reaching the "thoughtful" community which ponders serious matters on Sunday morning rather than spending time on less important matters, like worship.

Some years ago when President Jimmy Carter was traveling in South Korea he held a lengthy conversation with the South Korean president on the subject of religion. Carter spoke of his Baptist faith, and the South Korean president, nominally a Buddhist, listened with interest. When the news of this discussion leaked out, the *New York Times*, that staunch defender of secularity, chastised Carter for attempting to "proselytize" the South Korean. The *Times* editorial implied that there is something wicked about holding a conversation on faith, since it might lead to conversion.

The national opinion-shapers don't dislike religion. Rather, they're programmed by a common cultural wisdom that for two centuries has celebrated the intellect over the heart. That conventional wisdom respects religion, in its place, but it does not trust religious commitment as the basis for national thought or as a perspective underlying public discourse. Indeed, to gain intellectual respectability, it is best to avoid discussing religion, especially if that discussion involves what we Methodists refer to as a "witness." One can see the same mind-set at any gathering of the American Academy of Religion, the group of academics who teach religion in public and private colleges and universities. The greatest fear you sense in the corridors, apart from the fear of not landing a job, is that a professor might be suspected of harboring a genuine religious commitment in the midst of all that intellectual conversation.

Or consider Tim Robbins's comments in speaking to an interviewer at the Berlin Film Festival about a film he directed, *Dead Man Walking*: "I believe in . . . er . . . that there are . . . er . . . that there are people who are on earth who live highly enlightened lives and who achieve a certain level of spirituality, in connection with a force of goodness. And because these people have walked the earth, I believe that these people have created God." Though his film is an eloquent testimony to the power of a nun's religious faith, he himself is hesitant to speak about religion as anything more than an offshoot of secular morality. I find more truth in his film than in his testimony to a secularized spirituality.

Or consider the report by Caryn James in the *New York Times* on the recent Sundance Film Festival, in which she describes the film *Care of the Spitfire Grill* as "a manipulatively heartwarming story about a young woman just out of prison who finds spiritual redemption." James records that the movie "won the feature film audience award and was sold to Castle Rock Entertainment for $10 million." She goes on: "No one seemed to notice that it was financed by a conservative Mississippi company affiliated with the Roman Catholic Church and founded, as its 'mission statement' puts it, to 'present the values of the Judeo-Christian tradition.' The new company, called Gregory Productions, put up the $6 million for the film, set in a town called Gilead. Gregory is an offshoot of the nonprofit Sacred Heart League, which publishes inspirational literature."

James comments that the film "resembles an 'after school special' about forgiveness. But watching it with the Sacred Heart League in mind makes all the biblical imagery seem slightly sinister. When Marcia Gay Harden takes the heroine to mediate in a deserted church, it's hard to forget where the movie's money comes from. The director, Lee David Zlotoff, is Jewish and, he says, extremely religious. But the movies's multidenominational roots—Catholic backers, Protestant characters and a Jewish director—don't diminish the eerie sense that viewers are being proselytized without their knowledge."

Proselytized? Of the more than 600 movies released in this country each year, a substantial number of them are "guilty" of proselytizing on behalf of a worldview that celebrates greed, trivializes violence and winks at sexual activity among people of all ages at all times. Yet a movie that impressed a secular audience is found guilty of proselytizing because it has a clear religious perspective and origin. Such is the bias among our cultural leaders against religious faith as a basis for rational discourse.

FOOLISH WISDOM

In the matter of Supreme Court Justice Antonin Scalia and the *Washington Post*, we stipulate that compassion be shown to Joan Biskupic, a *Post* writer who reported on Scalia's April 9 speech in Mississippi on religion and public life. Using secondhand accounts, without a full text of the original speech, Biskupic reported that Scalia "delivered an ardent defense of religious beliefs against the assaults of secular society." In "unusually sharp remarks for a Supreme Court justice," Biskupic went on, Scalia said "the modern world dismisses Christians as fools for holding to their traditional beliefs." She quoted Scalia as saying that "we are fools for Christ's sake," and apparently didn't recognize that Scalia was citing a biblical passage (1 Cor. 4:10).

Less compassion is required for a subsequent *Post* story on the Scalia talk, written by Clay Chandler. Drawing on several legal figures,

Chandler informs readers of the "fierce debate" that Scalia's "scathing indictment of American society as dominated by secular 'worldly wise' enemies of Christianity" has provoked. "At issue is whether Scalia's impassioned and remarkably personal defense of Christianity" clashes with "his sworn duty to impartially interpret U.S. laws, including those pertaining to religion."

For a "Supreme Court justice to express himself so freely on religious matters is unequaled in the modern era," observed Stephen Gillers, a professor of legal ethics at New York University Law School, one of many alarmed respondents cited by Chandler. The reporter says that while "legal experts said the First Amendment grants Supreme Court justices, just like any other U.S. citizen, the right to speak their mind," other experts insist that "Scalia's comments were difficult to reconcile with his judicial obligation to regard citizens of all religious persuasions—whether believer or unbeliever, Christian or non-Christian—as equals under the law."

Elliot Mineberg, legal director for People for the American Way, was troubled by Scalia's remarks "because they so closely resemble those used by Christian activists such as Pat Robertson and Patrick Buchanan, who have asserted that the country is rife with anti-Christian bigotry." For Mineberg, "this is a disturbing view for a Supreme Court justice to have. This suggests a certain worldview that reads things that are designed to protect religious liberty—such as keeping church and state separate—as being anti-Christian."

An "attorney and ethics expert" who asked not to be identified told Chandler he was "shocked" by Scalia's remarks. He shouldn't "be saying anything like that because it's going to come up before the court. If he's got anything to say about religion or anything else, he should say it in his opinions. Those are the rules."

The tenor of Chandler's report suggests that Scalia's remarks somehow represent a threat to judicial order. But why should the worldview of a devout Catholic be more threatening than that of a thoroughly secular-minded justice?

Chandler points out that Washington State Supreme Court Justice Richard Sanders "provoked a political uproar in his state by addressing an antiabortion rally on the steps of the state capitol." In defending his actions, Sanders pointed to the career of Justice William O. Douglas, who served on the U.S. Supreme Court from 1939 to 1975. Well known as an environmental activist, Douglas wrote several books on the topic and frequently participated in public demonstrations of his commitment to preserving the environment. Sanders also cited the oft-stated civil rights positions of the late Justice Thurgood Marshall, who like Douglas was called upon to vote on cases that concerned issues that were personally important to him.

The most uncomprehending comments from the *Post* were those of columnist Richard Cohen, who denounced Scalia as a "cheap-shot artist" for his attack on the *Post*'s coverage of reported miracles in Virginia, and claimed Scalia was "abusing" the newspaper to make his point that the "worldly wise" are hostile "to religion and religious phenomena." He quoted Scalia as saying, "We are fools for Christ's sake. We must pray for the courage to endure the scorn of the sophisticated world." Cohen commented: "I will not quarrel with Scalia's self-assessment, although the cause of his foolishness is something only he himself can know." Once again, the reporter seemed to miss the point of Scalia's use of 1 Corinthians.

Scalia's remarks are not subversive. They are an honest expression of his belief in miracles and especially in the miracle of Christ's resurrection, and of his sense of how Christians should react to a culture that denigrates that faith.

The coverage of Scalia's speech, according to Robert A. Sirico, a Catholic priest who is president of the Acton Institute for the Study of Religion and Liberty in Grand Rapids, Michigan, "illustrates the very point he was making: The 'worldly wise' disparage religious belief and believers." Writing in the *Wall Street Journal*, Sirico offers this Pauline interpretation of Scalia's comments—an interpretation that the justice's critics have either deliberately ignored or failed to comprehend: "St. Paul's remark about himself and the other apostles being 'fools for Christ's sake' was meant to draw the contrast with the haughty and self-satisfied. It was a remark born of humility when faced with God's power over our lives. Contrary to the protests against Justice Scalia's speech, a responsible use of judicial reasoning, as well as intellectual objectivity, would seem to require such humility."

PLACING ONESELF

White male southern-born Americans are not high in the polit-ically correct lexicon these days. Nothing particularly wrong with that, of course, since white males born in any locale have controlled the power structures far too long. President Clinton's first Supreme Court nominee, a female jurist distinguished for her work in women's rights, is a solid PC appointment, but also a good choice on merit. The president is himself a WMSBA, but his Georgetown and Oxford education connected him early on to the eastern elite, which is why so many FOBs (Friends of Bill) are PC-sensitive easterners.

The president is a Southern Baptist, which is as much a cultural as a religious description. But as Shaun Casey writes in a report on "the president's religion" for the Nieman Foundation (*Nieman Reports*), Clinton's exposure to Catholic theology at Georgetown introduced him to "certain strains of Catholic social teaching, which he continued to cultivate throughout his adult life." Casey quotes from Clinton's 1992 speech at Notre Dame: "I loved the Catholic understanding of history and tradition and how they shape us."

Future historians will want to take note of Clinton's decision to make his only major address on religious values during the 1992 campaign at what many regard as the heart of American Catholicism. This could have been the result of a campaign decision to appeal to urban Catholic voters, but more likely it was due to Clinton's sense that his political orientation has at least as much to do with such Catholic social themes as (in Casey's words) "community, the need to balance rights and responsibilities, opportunities and obligations, and working for the common good" as it does with the tradition of Baptist theology.

Casey has a great deal more to say about how Clinton blends southern piety with Catholic doctrine, but what especially caught my attention was a reference to *Thinking in Time: The Uses of History for*

Decision Making, by Richard Neustadt and Ernest May. These two authors, notes Casey, emphasize the importance of "placing [a] person under scrutiny against public, historical events, and against what they call the relatively small details of personal history." Casey's motive in "placing" Clinton in both his early years as a Southern Baptist and in his college years in a Catholic university is to caution journalists against assuming that everything Clinton says and does must be understood as part of a Southern Baptist cultural and religious perspective. (Otto Hentz, a priest and professor of philosophy at Georgetown, who along with another priest, Joseph Sebes, were two of Clinton's favorite teachers, recalls that the future president's work in class led him to suggest to Clinton that he become a Jesuit.)

All of us have the need to relate "public, historical events" to the "relatively small details" of our own personal history. That is why I traveled recently to Fredericksburg, Virginia, to do some research on a great-great uncle who, according to family records, died in the Civil War battle at Chancellorsville. I knew very little about this man, except where he died, even though my early years were spent in a small Georgia county seat with the inevitable Confederate monument on the courthouse lawn. The inscription on that monument reads:

> On Fame's eternal camping ground,
> Their silent tents are spread,
> And Glory guards with solemn round,
> The bivouac of the dead.

Until I read that inscription recently in a Georgia travel book, I did not recall having previously seen those words, which are from a poem honoring Kentucky volunteers in the Mexican war. (The poem, "The Bivouac of the Dead," by Theodore O'Hara, begins with the more familiar line, "The muffled drum's sad roll has beat the soldier's last tattoo.")

What makes us notice some things and ignore others? As a child I passed that monument almost daily. Why wasn't I curious as to the source of its poetic inscription? Could it be that the Confederacy was something my parents wanted to forget? It wasn't until a few years ago, still uneasy over being a southern white male in a PC culture, that I began researching family history. One of the more interesting discoveries was the fact that my great-grandmother's two brothers,

James M. Tucker and John F. Tucker, died fighting in the war that is memorialized on that Monroe, Georgia, courthouse lawn.

Their father, McKendree Tucker, and their grandfather, Eppes Tucker, were both Methodist ministers and part of the Methodist Protestant denomination that broke with the Methodist Episcopal Church over the right of the laity to vote in episcopal elections. But they were also on the losing side of a war, and my part of the family heard very little about how both men had been killed in their early 20s. Many southerners of my generation have talked or written about relatives who regaled them with laments over the defeat, and recall evidence of a bitterness that lingered well into the 20th century. But not my family.

It was this veil of silence and the need to find my own personal "placement" that prompted me to find out what I could about the death of John F. Tucker, who, according to a memoir written by his uncle Coke Tucker in 1899, "was killed in the battle of Chancellorsville." That battle, fought a few days after the battle at Fredericksburg in early May 1863, when Lee drove the northern army back across the Rappahannock River, was considered Lee's military high point. It was also an event of horrible hand-to-hand combat in which the South lost 14,000; the North, 17,000 dead or missing.

My generation was not unaware of the Civil War, but I viewed the war as impersonal history, not as a collection of moments that shaped my life and that of my children. As a certified liberal and loyal follower of political correctness, I did not find it easy to re-enter an era in which the central reality was slavery. As I drove to Fredericksburg I pondered the question: Is it possible to reassemble the emotions of the past by linking oneself with a specific participant of that past? This was my chance to find another dimension of personal "placement," but I had to do so by revisiting the southern side of the Civil War (or, as the lady in the Virginia state library called it, with a perfectly straight face and a deep Virginia accent, "The War of Rebellion").

Barbara Tuchman quotes George Macaulay Trevelyan describing the historian as one who combines evidence of the past with "the largest intellect, the warmest human sympathy and the highest imaginative powers." The historian gathers facts, and then must "exercise the artist's privilege of selection" to deal with the "why" of what happened. And "sympathy is essential to the understanding of motive."

My visit to northern Virginia was the journey not of the historian, but of a family member who also wonders "why" and looks for whatever facts are available on the death of Martha Tucker's brother and McKendree Tucker's son 130 years ago. And this nonhistorian, recalling the Confederate monument of his childhood, was determined to do so with sympathy and imagination.

Government archives at Fredericksburg listed a John F. Tucker as a member of Alabama's 14th Infantry Regiment, one of several volunteer units assigned to the brigade commanded by General Cadmus Marcellus Wilcox. Knowing the name of a military commander is crucial in such research. Ernest B. Furgurson's *Chancellorsville, 1863: The Souls of the Brave* records that Wilcox's brigade fought at Salem Church, which served as both a southern battle station and a field hospital during the heavy fighting. The small brick structure still stands. According to Furgurson, "Wilcox's Alabamians and Semmes's Georgians play[ed] the major role in throwing back" the Union advance.

A small publication in the Richmond state library lists John Tucker of Chambers County, Alabama, as "missing" after the battle. I intend to see if anything else can be discovered from the Veterans Administration. I presume John died somewhere near a small Baptist church in northern Virginia, since that was the area to which his unit was assigned.

It is hardly politically correct to make much of one's Confederate heritage, but somehow I think I owe it to John F. Tucker, his sister Martha, and all the other Tuckers who one day in the late spring of 1863 received word of John's death, news that hit doubly hard since his older brother, James M. Tucker, had been killed six months earlier at the battle of Stones River near Murfreesboro, Tennessee. A visit to the place where war claimed the life of John F. Tucker, private, Confederate Army, 14th Alabama Infantry Regiment, was for me an important "though relatively small" detail of personal history.

And reclaiming the memory of John Tucker leads me to suggest that while Bill Clinton has been politically correct in his appointments, he would add to his effectiveness as a leader if he would also stay in touch with his own personal history. He is Georgetown and Oxford, but he is also Hope, Arkansas. It is not always easy being a southern white male, but we can't escape our personal history, and we shouldn't try to.

THE FREE PLAY OF THOUGHT

Matthew Arnold, the 19th-century British poet and critic, aimed, in Morris Dickstein's words, "to direct a free play of thought onto subjects that had become petrified by received opinion." Arnold believed that the critic should, in his memorable phrase, see life steadily and see it whole. Indeed, for Arnold, the welfare of the nation depended on citizens' ability to rise above personal, political and practical considerations and exercise a disinterested, critical point of view. This view of the critic sounds quaint in today's commercial culture. Even since the *New York Times* hired conservative pundit William Safire to bring "balance" to its pages, columnists have sought not to be judicious but to stridently represent a particular political—or ethnic or social—viewpoint.

Stridency and passion are also the driving forces behind the influential radio and television talk shows. These arbiters of discussion employ blatant distortion of history, Alice in Wonderland definitions of facts, character assassination and the demonization of opponents; they turn our public conversation into hostile shouting matches.

There is no such thing, of course, as completely disinterested or objective criticism. All criticism reflects the position and sensibility of the critic. Still, as Arnold emphasized, society needs criticism that aspires to transcend immediate practical and political considerations.

Arnold's view of culture was filtered through poetry and literature, but it was ultimately human conduct, not art, that concerned him. According to Dickstein, Arnold thought that "culture is conduct, or at least a firmer, more thoughtful ground on which conduct could be based" (*Double Agent: The Critic and Society*). "Culture is 'a study of perfection' which 'moves by the force, not merely or primarily of the scientific passion for public knowledge, but also of the moral and social passion for doing good.'" Arnold was, "above all, a diagnostic critic who uses literature instrumentally, to advance social health and human wholeness."

A random sampling of the so-called big news stories of recent months offers little that is of value in the advancement of social health and human wholeness. Did we, for example, need the extensive coverage of the bizarre and sad mass suicides of the Heaven's Gate community? Was the social significance of that event of such magnitude that *Newsweek* needed to devote almost half its editorial pages to the phenomenon? Did we really need to receive such massive daily doses of the two trials of O. J. Simpson? The coverage of and commentary on these and similar stories has everything to do with profitability and very little to do with the advancement of social health and human wholeness.

Bill Clinton and Newt Gingrich are supposed to be conducting the business of the people, but neither man can focus for long on his tasks without being reminded by our noisy cultural critics that the most important things about their lives is their misconduct in the past. Clinton and Gingrich have records that need to be examined and issues that need to be resolved, but what we see on a daily basis is neither news we can use nor information we need. It is more like gossip, peddled to a public far more interested in Paula Jones than in what cuts in food stamps are doing to poor children.

In *Breaking the News: How the Media Undermine American Democracy* (Pantheon, 1996), James Fallows writes that "journalism is not mere entertainment. It is the main tool we have for keeping the world's events in perspective. It is the main source of agreed-upon facts we can use in public decisions." But journalism has become a form of entertainment. Fallows cites Fred Wertheimer on the influence of television talk shows: "If I look at it from the standpoint of a TV talk show producer, a 'good journalist' is someone who has 'energy.' You hear this all the time. So and so has energy or doesn't have energy. It means someone who is noisy, opinionated, conflictual."

Fallows recalls a time when it wasn't this way. After World War II, he suggests, "people with a strong connection to academic life played the role of 'village explainer' in America." These explainers addressed the nation's new role in world affairs, the threats and possibilities of the atomic age, racial segregation and the importance of emerging technologies.

Vannevar Bush, for example, a former president of MIT and director of the government's Office of Scientific Research and

Development during the war, published an influential article in the *Atlantic Monthly* which "offered an amazingly prescient view of the effect of science on the world economy and of computers in daily life." Other articles written for general consumption in the postwar era came from such eminent figures as Arthur Schlesinger Sr., Richard Hofstadter, Henry Steele Commager and C. Vann Woodward. Public dialogue in that period was not without its frivolous and shallow stories—products such as hula hoops were duly noted—but, Fallows contends, attention was also paid to serious discussion of developments that would affect public policy.

Now the rule "No conflict, no news" governs cultural criticism. Shouting matches on television, and policy discussions viewed as games to be won or lost, set the standard for discussion. This leaves the public not only ill-prepared to make decisions, but also delivers us into the hands of profit-making commercial powers who are more than eager, in Neil Postman's perceptive phrase, to "amuse us to death."

CHANGES IN ATTITUDE

In a study of "the forgotten virtues of community" journalist Alan Ehrenhalt looks at three Chicago-area communities between the 1950s and the 1990s: a Catholic parish in the city, an African-American section of the South Side, and the suburb of Elmhurst. The thesis of his book, *The Lost City*, is that three major shifts in attitude have taken place since the 1950s. Understanding these changes can help us grasp movements in our culture, especially the rise of the Religious Right and its impact on the politics of 1996.

The first change Ehrenhalt identifies is a new attitude toward choice: choice today is universally considered a good thing; the more choices we have, the better. Second, authority is inherently suspect; we think nobody "should have the right to tell others what to think or how to behave." Third, sin is regarded as a social, not a personal, matter.

In the '50s, Ehrenhalt argues, the number of choices available were limited, and when a choice was made—the choice of a spouse or a vocation, for example—people were much more likely to remain loyal to their initial decision. Commitment was a virtue greatly honored, even when the choices made proved to be less than ideal. Manufacturing plants were reluctant to move to new areas for purely economic reasons.

Authority figures were not always loved in the 1950s, says Ehrenhalt, but they were still presumed capable of offering guidance. And, according to Ehrenhalt, who is the editor of *Governing* magazine, sin was still a viable category that referred to personal wrongdoing, the violation of a biblical code. The Ten Commandments were commandments, not suggestions, and they were frequently posted in public school classrooms.

Ehrenhalt presents one especially startling example of how different the world of the '50s was from that of today. He notes that in Elmhurst in the '50s one organization "stood far above all others as a symbol of fellowship and civic pride—the Jaycees, then known officially as the United States Junior Chamber of Commerce . . . the nerve center of the new suburban generation."

It was the Jaycees who revived the moribund Elmhurst Fourth of July celebration, with a parade, a fireworks display, a freedom flame pageant and an Iwo Jima tableau. They held a soapbox derby, and bused children from school to the circus on a Friday afternoon each spring. In December the Jaycees launched a "Put Christ Back in Christmas" campaign, crusading against the "Xmas" vulgarization and the creeping secularism it represented. In the winter of 1953, there were "Put Christ Back in Christmas" stickers and signs all over Elmhurst—on postal machines, on bushes, on every tree sold for the holidays anywhere in town. Residents were urged to send only cards that had a religious theme, and merchants were pressured to place biblical scenes in their stores' windows. The Boy Scouts were enlisted to distribute 8,000 pamphlets door-to-door, explaining the significance of the crusade.

Religion, specifically the religion that resented the vulgarization of "Xmas," was as much a part of the culture as the soapbox derby and the Fourth of July parade. This was the decade in which the words "under God" were added to the Pledge of Allegiance. President Eisenhower, who had never been a church member until he decided to run for the presidency (he quickly became a Presbyterian), summed up the religiosity of the period when he said: "Our government makes no sense unless it is founded on a deeply felt religious belief—and I don't care what it is."

Forty years later, secularity, not religiosity, is the dominant sensibility in public life. Putting Christ back into Christmas may still be a challenge to American churches, but today if anyone were to propose such a task to the Jaycees, they would respond with the bemused disbelief a city council would express if asked to sponsor an Easter sunrise service in city hall. We called it "religion in general" in the 1950s, and though it was merely a pious veneer over the culture, it nevertheless represented a very different sensibility from that of today.

In the past 40 years Americans have come to understand that they are a people of many religions and beliefs. This embrace of pluralism has been led by liberals whose benchmark belief has been tolerance. The American Civil Liberties Union has been in the forefront of fighting for tolerance and has served as the watchdog for signs that the nation's historic and numerically dominant faith—Christianity—is receiving preferential treatment. Not only do the Jaycees no longer push the cause of Christ in Christmas, but the baby Jesus himself has disappeared, along with his manger, from department stores and city property. Christians are still the dominant religious group, but it is no longer considered appropriate to proclaim one's religious faith in public settings. Ethics and morality have been cut off from their religious sources.

The Religious Right represents one response to these various developments. It seeks in some respects to return us to the ethos of the 1950s—an ethos of commitment, respect for authority, and concern for individual sin. It also seeks to restore public displays of religiosity.

The Religious Right arrived on the political scene in concert with the triumphs of political conservatism. The political revolution that brought conservatives to power began in its modern form in 1960, when Barry Goldwater failed is his attempt to gain the Republican Party's presidential nomination. Four years later Goldwater was the nominee, and though he lost the election to Lyndon Johnson, the conservative movement began to assume control of the Republican Party. By 1980 the movement was strong enough to choose a conservative nominee for president. The term "moderate Republican" has become, except in isolated instances, an oxymoron.

The rise of the Religious Right was fueled by three major Supreme Court decisions that altered traditional patterns of American life. First came *Brown v. Board of Education* (1954), which outlawed segregation in the public schools; second came the last in a series of cases banning recited prayer in public schools, *Engle v. Vitale* (1962); and third was *Roe v. Wade* (1973), which opened the way for legalized abortion.

In 1964 Jerry Falwell was a Virginia pastor who insisted during the civil rights controversy that religious people should stay out of politics and focus entirely on spiritual matters. But by 1980 Falwell had been converted to political action. He founded the Moral Majority, the precursor of today's Christian Coalition, formed by Pat Robertson. Robertson lost his own bid for the presidency in 1988, but as in the case of Barry Goldwater in 1964, out of that loss came a movement. Today that movement is spearheaded by the Christian Coalition.

The strength of the coalition may be measured in part by the fact that every major Republican presidential candidate wanted to appear at its 1995 annual meeting. Neither the Republican presidential nor vice-presidential nomination will be decided without support from the Christian Coalition. The coalition holds the kind of veto power that big-city mayors, African-American leaders and labor unions hold in the Democratic Party.

One response to this movement rooted in "traditional religious values" would be to dismiss it as a return to the Know-Nothing populism of the 19th century. That would be a mistake. As John Diggins points out in *The Lost Soul of American Politics*, the public longs to recover a sense that its members live under the guidance of a transcendent moral center, and they want to utilize such a center as an anchor from which they can exercise their democratic freedoms.

Jewish and Christian traditions have shaped who we are as a people. Embracing a narrow specificity, however, is an inappropriate way to celebrate that tradition, and such narrowness is the fundamental flaw in the Religious Right. When the Religious Right speaks of morality, it has a very parochial viewpoint in mind, a morality derived from an evangelical Protestant worldview with a heavy emphasis on a literal and at times apocalyptic interpretation of scripture.

The best response to the Religious Right, therefore, is to acknowledge that it is correct in believing that secularism does not deserve to be our enforced national faith. But a fundamentalist and parochial Christianity is not the answer to our quest for a moral center. In seeking for the lost soul in politics we need to respect the passions and commitments of the various religious traditions in this land.

QUESTIONS OF RIGHT AND WRONG

"The extreme individualism of middle-class religion, in the past two centuries, has narrowed the religious vision to the individual life, and made personal immortality and perfection the sole goal of religious striving. . . . It is very probable that the political means necessary for the achievement of a just society have never been clearly envisaged by any religion."

Reinhold Niebuhr

MAKING CHOICES ABOUT THE FINAL EXIT

A book about how to commit suicide has vaulted to the top of the best-seller lists. *New York Times* columnist Anna Quindlen admits that she picked up *Final Exit* out of curiosity, but kept it for another reason. The day may come when she will want to know how to die with a minimum of pain and anguish. And if that day does come, "whose business is it, really, but my own and that of those I love?" Derek Humphry's little volume went unnoticed until it was highlighted in the *Wall Street Journal*. Then media coverage was immediate and widespread, pushing the book to the top of the *Times* best-seller list.

Most commentators make the usual demurs, reminding us that the choice to die should be made in discussions with loved ones and professional counselors. And they point out that teenagers and adults despondent over temporary—or even permanent—burdens are not the book's intended audience. Only the terminally ill who face prolonged and painful suffering should be encouraged to prepare for the time when, as Quindlen says, "I may feel so bereft of strength, purpose, stamina and the will to live that I may want to know what constitutes a lethal dose of Seconal."

The issue here is clearly one of controlling how and when one dies—the understandable longing of the human spirit to name the time and place for a final exit. In our secular culture this seems an entirely reasonable desire, one which deserves fulfillment. But the desire to take one's own life is the epitome of modern individualism. If one thinks ultimate reality is located no higher than human personality, what one does with one's life is one's own affair. Betty Rollin, who wrote an introduction to *Final Exit*, is a television journalist who assisted in the suicide of her mother, who was terminally ill from ovarian cancer. Rollin argues that "some people want to eke out every second of life—no matter how grim—and that is their right." But others, she insists, do not, and "that should be their right."

But is it? When Quindlen maintains that her death is her business and that of "those I love," she does not consider the significance of suicide on the wider circles of life that surround her. John Donne's reminder that none of us is an island speaks to the point: the death of each individual has a ripple effect in the present and into the future.

If, as modernity dictates, the individual is supreme, then our responsibility is only to ourselves, since there is no God who gave us life or who awaits us in death. But if we believe that life derives from a loving Creator, then suicide must be considered within a larger context. In a nonreligious culture, *Final Exit* assures people that, in the face of death, individual choice is all that matters. Only someone who accepts individualism as the highest good would be so confident that there is an obvious qualitative difference between the "freely chosen" decision to die made by a person facing a terminal illness and a decision made by a physically healthy but mentally tormented individual.

In considering the "right to die," it is important to distinguish between the comatose patient being kept alive by mechanical means and the person still capable of making decisions. When consciousness disappears permanently, a decision to die becomes the responsibility of others, who may reach the judgment that for all practical purposes life for an individual has concluded and that therefore artificial supports need not be maintained.

Richard Lamm, the former governor of Colorado who has campaigned against excessive medical costs, recently cited the case of a patient in a Washington, D.C., hospital who has been in a comatose state since Lamm was a high school student. The patient has survived entirely through artificial means in a condition which benefits neither that person nor society. In this case, the larger community has not acted in the best interest of either the individual or the community. Fear of political and legal retribution from "right to life" activists has forced the medical community to preserve the person's life. That decision reflects a narrow definition of "life" held by a small but politically strong group of activists.

An individual does have the "right to die" when individual choice has disappeared and the decision on life or death has fallen to the community (primarily the family). That is why it is so important to instruct one's family in advance not to employ excessive means to sustain life when there is no prospect of recovering consciousness.

But what about a conscious decision to commit suicide? Though an individual may rationalize that his or her death would be to everyone's advantage, suicide leaves a void in a network of close relationships. Its impact does not stop with "those I love." Friends, former teachers, colleagues, distant family relations, even casual acquaintances are all affected by suicide. The web of life, as Joseph Sittler so aptly put it, is like a spider web: touch any part, and the entire web shimmers.

Despite Humphry's caveats and warnings, his book is irresponsible. There is, admittedly, a difference between the elderly terminal patient in horrible pain who wants all pain to cease and the despondent teenager whose pain is one of low self-esteem. But the difference is finally one of degree. The terminally ill person, out of personal suffering and a concern for the impact a lingering illness has on family and the immediate human circle, may turn to suicide. But the emotionally distraught teenager or adult may reach the same conclusion: my pain is too great, and my presence is detrimental to those around me. To make that decision before life involuntarily leaves us is a decision we are free to make, but it is a choice that is ultimately selfish. It is not surprising that our culture, which regards individual choice as inviolable, would find so much merit in a book like *Final Exit*.

SUICIDE, RESPONSIBILITY
AND THE SACREDNESS OF LIFE

____

Derek Humphry's *Final Exit,* a celebration of the right to die—and a guide to how to do it—set off a furious national debate among both secularists and religionists. My recent characterization of the book as irresponsible set off a storm of mail from *Century* readers, many of whom believed I had overlooked the agonizing decisions facing the terminally ill and their families.

In my effort to argue that suicide is an individual act of selfishness that negates one's responsibility to the human community, I did slight the suffering of those in their final days or hours when death is imminent and pain is intolerable. Those who have witnessed family members in those final hours, and others who anticipate their own last moments, were understandably disturbed by what they perceived as my insensitivity to the terminally ill.

In discussing *Final Exit* I did suggest that while there is an obvious difference between "the elderly terminal patient in horrible pain who wants all pain to cease and the despondent teenager whose pain is one of low self-esteem," the difference is finally one of degree. It is on this "degree" that the debate should focus. And when the Hemlock Society produces a book that describes suicide methods in a favorable light, it becomes necessary to label suicide for what it is: individual self-centeredness. Yes, there is a marked difference between the suicide of a depressed teenager and a family's agreement that a terminally ill, elderly loved one is ready to exit life with everyone's best interest at heart.

Complex moral decisions made with the counsel of family, friends and medical professionals are of quite a different order from the lonely judgment reached by someone for whom life is "no longer worth living." A desire to be pastorally responsible in assisting terminally ill individuals must not ignore the religious imperative that human life is the sacred responsibility of both individual and community.

Humphry recently clarified his own opposition to suicide when it is an escape from an unhappy life. He was moved to do so by the suicide of his former wife, a co-founder of the Hemlock Society, Ann Wickett Humphry. According to news reports from Bend, Oregon, Ann Wickett (her professional name) disappeared near Three Creeks Lake on the eastern border of the Three Sisters Wilderness Area. Police found her body several days later after an intensive search by hunters and other volunteers, according to Deschutes County Sheriff Darrell Davidson. (She did not die "in isolation." People looked for her; friends and family grieved over her loss; her horse was left to wander in the wilderness; and her death is now precipitating even further discussion of the cause she had long advocated.)

Humphry said police told him that Wickett had left a suicide note at her home. Humphry also said that while Wickett had had breast cancer, he thought the malignancy has been removed and he was not aware of any recurrence. Humphry and Wickett had collaborated on *Jean's Way*, an account of the assisted suicide of Humphry's first wife, and on a second book, *The Right to Die: Understanding Euthanasia*. Earlier Wickett had written *Double Exit*, a description of the double suicide of her aged parents.

According to an Associated Press report, Humphry and Wickett divorced in 1990 "after a highly publicized bitter separation in which Ann Humphry contended that her husband abandoned her after learning that she had potentially life-threatening breast cancer." At the time of her death she was suing her former husband, "charging libel and slander for comments he made about her mental state."

In a paid advertisement in the *New York Times*, Humphry described his wife as a woman "of Nordic beauty, enormous talent . . . a gourmet cook and often wonderful company, [but] at other times her depressions were so serious that she had to be hospitalized." He added that "suicide for depression has never been part of the credo of the Hemlock Society" and that the society supports "suicide prevention in appropriate cases."

Readers who responded to my initial editorial on *Final Exit* understandably focused on the pastoral concerns involved with intense physical suffering from a terminal illness. And this is an important consideration in any discussion of how we confront dying. But this pastoral focus must not allow us to overlook the point that, as one respondent wrote me, "conscious decisions to commit suicide are likely to increase as a result of a sort of implicit permission that the very publication of Humphry's book has given, despite his 'caveats and warnings.'"

We will never know how Ann Wickett reached her decision to go into the wilderness of Oregon to take her own life. But we do know that she believed in the principle that suicide is a solution to the pain of life. In her case (assuming she believed herself cancer-free) it was not a terminal physical illness that led to suicide, but an emotional pain that she must have believed she could no longer endure.

The Humphry-Wickett campaign in favor of suicide has opened an important debate. It is one in which the religious community must take the side of the absolute sacredness of life, with a commitment to the principle that the life we are privileged to live is given to us by God. To be responsible stewards of life is not just a suggestion but an obligation. Our eagerness to be sensitive to the special circumstances surrounding terminal illness does not relieve us of our responsibility to God and to the network of relationships we are privileged to share.

POLITICS AND THE DARKNESS OF LYING

When George Bush announced his nomination of Clarence Thomas to the U.S. Supreme Court, he told the American people two things that almost no one believed: that race was not a factor in the selection, and that Thomas was the best-qualified person for the position.

There are certain situations in which we are permitted to fudge the truth. We may say that the gift of a necktie is just what we needed even though we have many more just like it at home. But when a president argues for a Supreme Court nominee it is expected that there will be a congruence between what he knows to be true and what he says is true.

The president's initial announcement set the standard for the hearings that followed, during which, under oath, Thomas told the Judiciary Committee that he had never discussed *Roe v. Wade*. No one believes that, including the 52 senators who voted to confirm Thomas. As Garry Wills noted in his syndicated column, "Now we have a perjurer on the bench." Wills went on to quote Robert Bork as saying there are only two people in America who have not talked about *Roe v. Wade*—David Souter and Clarence Thomas. Souter at least managed to evade the committee's questions on the subject, whereas Thomas said flat out that he had never discussed the case.

Evasions and lies have become de rigueur for Supreme Court nominees. Bork did not lie or evade in his response to questions, and he was rejected for being outside the "mainstream" of American opinion—which means he was outside the preference range of the advocacy groups who opposed him. Now that this principle has been established, liberal appointees can expect the same treatment from conservative groups.

When the Senate Intelligence Committee endorsed Robert Gates as the director of the Central Intelligence Agency, it did so despite Gates's association with former CIA chief William Casey, someone who was not always truthful in speaking to his aides or to the American people. Gates insisted he knew nothing of Casey's involvement in the Iran-contra affair, though officials below him in the hierarchy suggested otherwise. Questions about Gates's stewardship and his relationship to Casey were not considered sufficient to prevent confirmation. His experience in running the agency was more important for the senators than the "lesser issue" of truth-telling.

Lying has its advantages. I was involved some years ago in a lawsuit filed after our family dog bit someone. An investigator came by our house some weeks after the transgression and casually asked if this was the first time Rebel had bitten anyone. I was unaware that the law automatically condemns a dog for a "second bite," taking the view that once is a mistake but twice is a pattern. Three young boys were looking up at their father as he fielded the question. All of us knew that Rebel had, indeed, been guilty of an earlier transgression. We loved the dog and knew he was high-spirited, but not mean. Both bites, in our opinion, were innocent, not vicious acts. Since truth-telling is important in our family—and since I didn't know about the telling is important in our family—and since I didn't know about the two-bite rule—I mentioned the earlier incident. The investigator was delighted with the information. Our insurance company eventually settled out of court and we had to have Rebel put to death, an act that neither I nor the boys have ever forgotten or forgiven.

Lying sometimes may help us accomplish an immediate goal (like saving Rebel). But each lie undermines the network of trust on which relationships rely. Lying is wrong, furthermore, because it violates our covenant with God, a covenant that sustains us in our human frailty. Without a moral principle backing our daily intercourse, we are left to function with the utilitarian assumption that if it works, do it; if it feels good, try it. The bottom line, maximum return and cost efficiency become the trinity for those who assume there is no general moral principle by which we are meant to live.

Rollo May, writing in *The Cry for Myth*, notes that the 20th century was once heralded as the age in which education would enable society to embrace a "religion cleansed of all superstition," by which he meant any belief that went beyond rationality. But, May argues, our age has not been blessed by the anticipated benefits of rationalism. "As a people we are more confused, lacking in moral ideals, dreading the future, uncertain what to do to change things or how to rescue our own inner life."

One of the more memorable quotes from the Watergate era is from the wife of a White House staffer who opened her front door and found herself confronted by *Washington Post* reporters Bob Woodward and Carl Bernstein. Knowing their mission, she paused for a moment and then stated quietly, "This is an honest house." The answers her husband later proved indicated that their home was indeed one of the few connected to the scandal that could claim that distinction.

Near the end of the Sermon on the Mount is a word for a nation that rewards deception and honors lying: "The eye is the lamp of the body. So if your eye is sound, your whole body will be full of light; but if your eye is not sound, your whole body will be full of darkness. If then the light in you is darkness, how great is the darkness."

MORAL WISDOM AND SEXUAL CONDUCT
____

She is an attractive woman, dark hair pulled back in a bun (the way my mother used to wear hers), probably in her mid-40s. Well dressed, friendly and a bit exuberant, she reflects a sense of happiness and excitement rarely found in a seatmate on a crowded plane traveling to Chicago. I am hunched over my laptop computer, fighting a deadline with an intensity that usually would discourage conversation in this confined torture chamber high above the Rockies.

She wants to talk. I respond politely and continue to type. But she is persistent. So I listen. She is going to Chicago to meet her fiancé, who is flying in from New York. They will spend the weekend together in Chicago. She is a widow, he a widower. They had met several months ago and were now conducting a whirlwind cross-country courtship which would soon, she said with obvious glee, result in matrimony.

We talked about the things she and her fiancé could see and do in Chicago, but we didn't refer at all to morality, or chastity before marriage, or safe sex, since such matters should not be discussed between strangers. But the subject was on my mind because on the screen in front of me was the uncertain beginning of an editorial inspired by the discussion prompted by Earvin "Magic" Johnson's dramatic announcement that he is infected with the HIV virus.

I had initially been saddened by his immediate retirement from basketball—a loss to the sport and a much greater loss to him, as the virus leaves him vulnerable to AIDS, the disease from which no one has yet recovered. Which is why I am staring at the screen, trying for some clarity on the matter of Magic and sex as my seat companion expresses her happiness at finding the right man.

The initial adulation for Magic's "courage" has subsided somewhat, and a few questions are now being raised about his premarriage promiscuity. They are questions, however, that say as much about the inability of our society to deal with complex moral issues as they do about Magic's infection. Moreover, when he announced that his exposure to the virus came through heterosexual, not homosexual, contacts, he maintained his status as a sports hero—further indication of the uneasiness our society has with gay people. As his fellow sports star Martina Navratilova has noted, Johnson's public acceptance was guaranteed once he clarified this little detail about his sexual contacts. Navratilova, an acknowledged lesbian, correctly noted that had she made the same announcement, she would not have received such a positive response. "They'd say I'm gay—I had it coming," she said in an interview. Gay sex between committed partners is still out, while heterosexual promiscuity is in—provided, of course, it is practiced "safely."

Magic promises that he will be a spokesman on the subject of AIDS and the HIV virus. He will tell young people to be aware of the importance of safe sex, and always to use condoms when they participate in sexual activities. But it is what Magic has not said that should be the basis of our current national debate. He has not said to young people that sexuality is at the core of their personal identity and that sexual activity is not to be engaged in casually and without commitment.

It is not surprising that Magic has avoided such counsel and has continued to treat his extensive sexual contacts in such cavalier fashion. He is, after all, a product of a liberal culture with no moral compass with which to guide this debate. Our common life has become so thoroughly secular that faced with a danger as threatening as AIDS, we talk of preventive measures, not moral decision-making.

The attractive woman who sits beside me on the plane as I write is unable to see my screen, so she is unaware that she has changed the focus for a piece that has been troubling me for weeks. I wonder, without asking, what decision she and her fiancé have made for this coming weekend. They surely know about safe sex, for as Magic Johnson and others have pointed out, one of the side benefits of his announcement is the public attention now given to the use of condoms. The need for safe sex is out in the open and condoms may soon be advertised on television, sandwiched between the sex-saturated, titillating programs designed to appeal to the same teenagers who are hearing from Johnson that they should practice safe sex.

Columnist Ellen Goodman is one of those liberal opinion-shapers who is at a loss to offer guidance in what she terms the S.M. (Since Magic) era. "Most of us realize that premarital sex is here to stay," she writes—not a very profound observation, since it has been here to stay since Adam and Eve ate of the fruit of knowledge. The difference between our current situation and that abrupt departure from the innocence of Eden is the development of a pill that removed the fear of pregnancy, long a barrier to promiscuity. This medical achievement, coupled with the absence of a moral compass within our secular society, has given us the freedom to wander around outside Eden with little regard for the consequences of our sexual activity.

Now with our freedom under threat from a new fear, the best that liberal secular guides like Goodman can offer is a lament that the discussion is polarized around the "moralists" and the "medicalists"—one pushing monogamy, the other praising Magic as "a heterosexual poster child." In groping for an alternative to those two extreme options, Goodman asks us to "clarify our values" and "approve both condoms and caution." Values and caution based upon what principle to guide us? She does not say.

Even more poignant is columnist Anna Quindlen's promotion of safe sex with the outlandish assertion that she is less concerned with her child's lifestyle than with her child's life. Now there is a text for the end of the 20th century, a reductio ad absurdum of liberal secularity's elevation of individual freedom to ultimacy.

Quindlen was moved to her defense of survival over behavior by Vice-President Quayle's moralistic judgment against Magic Johnson, and in this she has a point. It is not Magic's promiscuity that is at issue here. She feels that the moralists—a category meant, I suspect, to encompass most religionists—are not much help in this debate. But those of us in the liberal religious community are also little help because we have been so fearful of the moralist label that we have no moral base from which to enter the debate.

The liberal religious community has felt helpless before the dramatically changing sexual mores of the final decade of the 20th century because we have allowed ourselves to remain trapped between the inflexible moralists on one side and the freedom-worshiping secularists on the other. We officially make noises like the moralists, knowing that such preachments are not effective in the face of secular calls to absolute freedom.

In one of those interesting accidents of timing only a few months before Magic Johnson put human sexuality on the national agenda, the Presbyterian Church (U.S.A.) tried to correct this institutional paralysis over sexuality when it considered a study document designed to confront the inadequacy of both an empty moralism and an arrogant secularity.

The Presbyterian study correctly linked sexuality with commitment and responsibility, and it tried to make clear that there is a distinction between teenage passion (felt by people of all ages) and mature commitment. The inherent ambiguity within such an enterprise is beyond the capacity of the media to comprehend, and as a result the document was pilloried by religious moralists and by secularists, both of whom assume that religion is supposed to condemn and control, not guide and sustain. Confronted with this dual attack, a confused and embarrassed Presbyterian General Assembly retreated from its honest attempt to search for the meaning of a religiously based sexual commitment.

Anna Quindlen is wrong. Lifestyle is life. How we live determines who we are. Mere survival is not sufficient to define a full life. Our religious tradition understands that our sexual conduct is at the heart of who we are. Let's be honest about this. Moses got the word on the mountain that if the Israelites were going to live in any kind of harmony with themselves and their God, they had to pay attention to the basics.

We are fragile creatures, inherently guilty, because in our self-centeredness we can never live fully on behalf of others—which is why we need guidelines surrounding our commitments. Without those guidelines we live only for the moment, giving little thought to possible consequences of our actions.

Which brings me back to the woman sitting beside me on this flight. I have no idea how she will conduct herself on her visit. Her fiancé has children in Chicago, so perhaps they will be well chaperoned. They may have chosen to abstain until they are married, or they may be expressing their love for one another in a more intimate manner. This is a private matter, and certainly not one for me to discuss with my seatmate in these final moments as the plane is landing.

But I do wonder how much longer our society will stay trapped in a futile debate on sexuality limited to the moralists and the medicalists, neither of whom has much sense of the moral wisdom, compassionate understanding and sense of ambiguity available to us from the biblical tradition.

The plane lands and I look again at the rather nervous but excited woman to my left. As I wish her well, I realize that I am also voicing a silent prayer for her future happiness. That is the least I can do. After all, she has helped me meet a deadline.

WHEN FREE SPEECH IS OFFENSIVE

Steve Dahl and Garry Meier are two radio talk show hosts whose outrageous insults and racy humor earn high ratings during drive time in Chicago. Commuters tune in to hear how far Dahl and Meier will push the boundaries of taste.

One evening not long ago, while on the topic of Catholic priests and child molestation, the pair went too far, at least for the Chicago chapter of the Catholic League for Religious and Civil Rights. After hearing reports of the broadcast, League executive director Tom O'Connell obtained a transcript of the exchange between Dahl and Meier and then wrote to the radio station's general manager, demanding an apology. He did not ask that Dahl and Meier be fired, nor did he suggest that they be censored. Instead, he wanted to meet with station officials to engage in some consciousness-raising. He wanted to force the station at least to consider the point at which speech becomes offensive and inappropriate.

In the exchange between Dahl and Meier tasteless remarks regarding child molestation were mixed with lighthearted references to the sacrament of communion, remarks which O'Connell found "bigoted and insensitive to the Catholic community," displaying "complete disrespect for the Holy Eucharist." The *Chicago Sun-Times* reported that in the reference to the Eucharist it was suggested that the "bread served at mass be switched to 'a little hot sausage' or 'bananas Foster.'" The paper added, "They also hinted at oral sex between a cardinal and an altar boy."

The freedom-of-speech clause in the First Amendment is meant to protect the most unattractive kinds of speech on the assumption that what offends one group could be a legitimate expression for others and may in time emerge as a truth that needed expression. In the interests of free debate our society tolerates a great deal of offensive speech, including not-so-subtle suggestions by politicians that people of different races or religion are inferior or dangerous. (Political candidate David Duke has built his career on offensive remarks directed at minorities. Now that his image is established, he has shifted from tasteless remarks to code words that suggest the same insults.)

Someone reading or hearing a sanitized version of that radio broadcast might conclude that the Catholic leaders were being overly sensitive, and perhaps were unnecessarily exercising their clout to intimidate the media. And since the issue of child molestation is an important one—particularly in the archdiocese of Chicago, which has recently had to admit its failure to police sexual offenders among the priesthood—it might seem that the exchange was appropriate. But it is difficult to examine the text without concluding that what was broadcast to commuters and families getting ready for supper was an expression of contempt for a particular religious belief.

Consider these excerpts: "Garry was an altar boy—he might—I bet he's got a story he can unpack on us but he can't work it to the surface yet. He did kiss a guy's ring on his knees." "Then cardinal of Chicago." "Kiss it—kiss my jewelry." "Did confirmation at our church and I served under him." "Under his robe and the reward for that was I got to kneel down and kiss his big ring." "His big dirty smelly ring." "That was an honor." "And I bet he held it near his crotch too, didn't he—you like it down there, you like my jewelry down there, boy—huh, get down on your knees, boy—cardinal—and go get some more good wine—alright—well anyway—but nobody calls the cops—call cops, man, that's what you do—but the good news is less than 4 percent are pedophiles, of course [inaudible] mean less than 4 percent have gotten caught."

Radio personnel are supervised by station administrators who are responsible for the content of programs to owners and the public. Radio and television stations use airways that are leased to them by the federal government. The Federal Communications Commission was established to protect the public interest and to guide the way in which stations use the airways. A station's license is subject to revocation if the FCC determines it is not fulfilling its responsibility to the public.

When the FCC is vigilant, stations watch their language. Unfortunately, since the Reagan era appointees to the FCC have been less concerned with their monitoring function and have treated the airways as though they belong to the stations. One result of this FCC posture has been an increased use of offensive material by stations fighting for higher profits through ratings.

Does pressure from offended groups work? Can anyone imagine a radio station using this sort of language in connection with an African-American pastor or a Jewish rabbi? Those minorities have long been vigilant against slurs, and while they are still subject to insults in coded terms, overt remarks such as these aimed at Catholics are rarely heard.

After receiving O'Connell's letter demanding an apology, WLUP-AM General Manager Lawrence J. Wert arranged a meeting with representatives of the Catholic League. Later, Wert sent a letter to the League office, saying: "We deeply regret that you were offended by the treatment of issues related to Catholic doctrines on the Steve and Garry show. While WLUP-AM encourages free and open discussion on all controversial issues, we attempt to foster such discussion without offending any segment of our community. . . . As our regular listeners know, Steve and Garry often use humor as a primary means both to entertain and inform. Humor, particularly when extemporaneous, is not always funny to everyone." Acknowledging that he disagreed with the League's "characterization of our broadcast," Wert wrote that he rejected any intention of the station "to offend anyone in this way. Given your reaction to both sets of remarks . . . we do sincerely and deeply apologize." He added that "it is our belief that open discussion promotes religious freedom and tolerance."

O'Connell said he accepted the apology and hopes that "issues of this nature do not occur on WLUP or any other Chicago area media." Both the station and the Catholic League consider the matter closed. But the need for vigilance by religious communities remains. The station's remark about "open discussion" promoting "religious freedom and tolerance" is a corporate cop-out, a way to avoid confronting the gross nature of the remarks for which the station was apologizing. Meanwhile, the Dahl and Meier show continues to be one of the area's highest-rated programs—a sad commentary on both public taste and the station's lust for profit. So when we are offended, we should, following the Catholic League's example, protest firmly and loudly. That is not censorship. It is simply a smart way to participate in public debate.

WATER IN THE BASEMENT,
JUDGMENT IN THE FLOOD

I miss Richard John Neuhaus. Protestant conferences haven't been the same since the acerbic pastor left Lutheranism for the Roman Catholic priesthood. I don't miss his infuriating ability to clobber a debating opponent by citing obscure theologians or court rulings. What I do miss is his masterful use of apophasis.

Apophasis is the term for mentioning something by denying that it will be mentioned. ("I shall not mention Caesar's avarice, nor his cunning, nor his morality.") This device has long been a Neuhaus trademark. He can use apophasis like no one else. He might remark, for example: "I'm not going to say that this learned editor runs a magazine that is a wishy-washy, anemic, politically correct excuse for what a robust, red-blooded Christian publication ought to be. No, I'm not going to say that, though there are people out there who will say it."

Neuhaus's rhetorical gift came to mind recently while I was talking to the owner of our neighborhood deli, who was complaining bitterly about his loss of business since the Chicago River sprang a leak and flooded downtown subbasements. I heard myself replying, "I'm not going to suggest it, but I have heard it said that it may be more than just a coincidence that the flood came a few days after our mayor decided he wanted to bring gambling casinos into downtown Chicago. Fortunately, this time no one was injured or killed. Maybe this is just a first warning." Instead of hooting at my impudence, the deli owner responded seriously, "Reverend, if you have any influence, let's get this over with." The influence he had in mind was not in regard to City Hall.

Later, I felt guilty. I had asserted a position that I was not willing to claim in my own name. But I had heard someone speculate about the connection between the flood and gambling. I had been hearing it for several days from my frustrated muse, and that is what finally pushed me into what I believe was my first public use of apophasis.

Such a cause-and-effect theological observation is not tenable, of course. The city of Chicago is guilty of sins far worse than gambling, sins that under the rubric of cause and effect would have attracted divine attention long before the river sprang its leak. But it is tempting to make the link, if only as a metaphor. In the hope of bringing billions of dollars into the city, the mayor, the city council and local commercial leaders have been beating some loud drums in favor of establishing gambling casinos—thereby adding to the state's gambling mania, which is already at a high pitch thanks to a state lottery and offshore gambling boats on the Mississippi River.

Except for a strong objection raised by the area's United Methodist bishop, even the city's religious community has been distressingly silent. Which is why my frustrated muse kept arguing that something ought to be said, especially about the absurd statement by city leaders that the issue is no longer a moral one—that question having been settled long before. What is that supposed to mean? Is it now settled that gambling is a freely chosen form of entertainment, and that in a free society it is everyone's prerogative to place wagers?

Wrong. Gambling exploits a human weakness. Gambling parallels its constant companion, prostitution, in suggesting that one can buy happiness. When gambling is not only condoned but officially supported by city and state officials through lotteries and licensed parlors, then government has become a pimp for sin. What my frustrated muse has been urging me to say is that gambling is a sin for the theologically sound reason that anything that exploits human weakness denigrates God's creation and separates us from our creator.

It is hard to speak of sin and judgment because cause and effect is the lingua franca of our society, and the thought of a divine being punching a hole in the Chicago River in response to an official endorsement of gambling is ridiculous. We are all rationalists, dedicated to the proposition that when bad things happen, there must be a cause, like the failure of a few city employees to plug a slow leak before it became a torrent. To make God the "cause" is to denigrate God. I know all that.

I also know that in this secular environment we are not comfortable speaking of judgment because we are literalists, surface-oriented thinkers. We know that since no human parent would punish a child out of proportion to the misdeed committed, no divine parent would rain fire or water down on a sinful universe.

Which only illustrates how out of touch we are with a deeper understanding of divine wisdom and judgment. Just the other day, for example, I complimented a speaker on his use of a particular quotation. He replied that he had just stumbled across that quotation by accident just in time to include it in the talk. "It was almost as if I had been divinely guided," he said apologetically.

"Almost as if" is another form of apophasis. We can't really believe that God would guide our hand on paper. If we were to adhere to such a view, we would be left with the puzzle of why God doesn't guide us when we really need it, like the time we drove our car into a tree. But in believing there is a transcendent dimension we don't have to assume that every human occurrence is "caused" by that dimension. God is not limited by time and space, and there is such a thing as free will.

But as my frustrated muse wants me to make clear, we don't always have to say that we get insight "almost as if" we were guided in our search. It is just possible that in some strange way we *are* connected with that power who creates, sustains and, yes, guides us. So if you want to describe gambling as a sin and don't want to sound pietistic, just say that while you would not express it exactly this way, you have read someone else—who was claiming that a frustrated muse was his source—saying something about it.

THE BERNARDIN FACTOR

One of those significant paradigmatic moments that could reshape public attitudes may have occurred in the sensational charge of sexual abuse brought by a 34-year-old former preseminarian against Chicago's Cardinal Joseph Bernardin. The charge stems from Steven Cook's recollection of what he says was a "repressed memory" of a sexual encounter 17 years ago when Cook was 17 and Bernardin was archbishop of Cincinnati.

The cardinal, who immediately labeled the accusation "totally untrue," is one of the nation's most respected Catholic leaders. Bernardin's colleagues in the National Conference of Catholic Bishops have pledged their "full support" for him and have praised him as a man of integrity.

Cook's civil suit against the cardinal, seeking damages of $10 million, sets in motion a process that could take up to five years to complete. Cook has requested a jury trial, which means that Bernardin would eventually have to face his accuser in a courtroom unless he agrees to a settlement to halt the process—unlikely, because of the appearance of implied guilt that tends to accompany such a settlement—or unless Cook withdraws the suit—also unlikely, since one of Cook's attorneys, Steven Rubino of Ventnor, New Jersey, has made something of a career out of suing the Roman Catholic Church. (Rubino is the author of *Church as a Litigant*, described by the *Chicago Tribune* as a "veritable guidebook" for attorneys who want to file sexual-abuse suits against the Catholic Church.)

What is most regrettable in this incident is the damage done to Bernardin's reputation, and to the church in which he is a major leader. As Chicago attorney Cathy Pilkington, who began her career handling criminal cases, points out, "You cannot unring a bell." Pilkington sees in Bernardin's experience a parallel to the Salem witch trials of 1692-93, in which the court of the Massachusetts colony permitted "spectral evidence" to be used against people accused of witchcraft. Pilkington, a legal scholar who has studied the Salem witch trials, suggests that the use of "repressed memory"—Cook claims he recalled the incident under hypnosis—is not unlike the spectral evidence that eventually led to the 17th-century accusations against more than 100 people in the Massachusetts colony.

Testimony was permitted in those trials in which charges were made against defendants who allegedly had appeared in spirit form in their witching activities. Among those charged, 21 people met death as "witches"—19 women and men were hanged, one man was pressed to death by huge stones, and one woman died in prison. By 1711 the legislature of the Massachusetts colony reconsidered its earlier acceptance of spectral evidence and paid reparations to families of those executed as "witches."

Sexual abuse as an expression of power over children or vulnerable adults is finally receiving greatly needed public exposure. But the act of uncovering abuse can itself be abused. In addition, repressed memory as a tool in therapy receives mixed reviews within the helping professions. Bringing hidden memories to the surface has helped some people recall traumas from early childhood, but critics of the technique—a recent phenomenon in therapy, dating perhaps back to 1983—fear that some therapists may be inducing fictional memories in their patients, whether inadvertently or deliberately. In many cases, however, when the traumatic events are recalled and confrontation between the accused and accuser takes place, reconciliation and healing do occur.

Nonetheless, there is an important difference between the use of "repressed memories" in legal cases and their use as a therapeutic tool. Without corroborating evidence, the use of such recollections in the courtroom poses a threat to our current legal system not unlike the threat posed by the use of "spectral evidence" in the Salem witch trials.

Cardinal Bernardin's experience may be the case that highlights this technique sufficiently to put it in perspective. Steven Cook may have benefited from bringing into consciousness what he believes to be 17-year-old memories. He may be convinced that he is telling the truth, either because the event did occur or because his recollection is so strong that it "feels" true. There is also the possibility that, as critics of the technique contend, Cook was led to recall something that did not actually take place.

In any event, Cook insists that he is making the memory public in order to tell the truth and to relieve his pain. But he is interested in more than confronting his personal nightmares. Within a few weeks of remembering what allegedly happened to him at age 17, he filed a lawsuit, asking for $10 million in damages. While that act does not by itself discredit him—any citizen has a right to seek relief from personal injury—Bernardin's supporters understandably regard the suit as an act that at least raises a question of pecuniary interest on the part of Cook and his attorneys.

Beyond Bernardin's personal anguish, however—and Cook's need to find relief for what he claims was a personal injury—is the matter of the vulnerability of professionals like Bernardin, public figures whose work with individuals leads them into private interaction with parishioners, clients, patients and students. What could make the cardinal's experience a transforming moment in American culture is the combination of his high personal reputation for integrity and his long record of concern for those who have, in fact, suffered sexual abuse by priests; some months ago he established a panel to investigate such charges against priests in his own diocese—a panel that, ironically, will now examine the charges against him.

Instances of sexual abuse have all too often been suppressed. The increase in the number of cases brought to public attention, however, may in part be the result of what Charles Krauthammer has described in a *New Republic* article as "defining deviancy up"—the process whereby "once innocent behavior now stands condemned as deviant." But no doubt the increase in reported cases is also related to the much-needed spotlight thrown in recent years on behavior that ought to be condemned as deviant. Persons of power can and do take advantage of the young and vulnerable, and for far too long they have done so largely with impunity.

If spectral evidence has some value in therapy, it is still suspect as a method in law. And when leveled against public figures even nonspectral charges without a shred of merit receive extensive exposure through market-driven (as opposed to service-oriented) media. Bernardin's case offers the opportunity to re-examine legal and media processes to look for ways to protect not only those subject to sexual abuse, but also those in positions of power who are vulnerable to character assassination.

Protection against unwarranted allegations is not unknown in the system. Most states, for example, require that clients who claim misconduct on the part of an attorney and want his or her license removed must make that claim in a "sealed" allegation, presented to a state licensing agency. But a civil suit against an attorney or any other citizen is immediately placed on the public record, leading to situations in which individuals like Bernardin are forced to defend themselves through extended legal procedures—even as they automatically "lose" in the court of public opinion, smeared by implication regardless of the trial's final outcome.

Like Senator McCarthy going one step too far with Joseph Welch, or Ross Perot bristling too often against Al Gore, the Bernardin suit may be a defining moment that could lead state legislatures to consider the "Bernardin factor" and require that civil suits against those who work in the helping professions—clergy, teachers, doctors, lawyers, dentists—be temporarily sealed until proven to have sufficient merit to proceed. There is danger in sealing any legal action, but legislatures have a responsibility to protect both the strong and the weak. The cardinal's experience could lead to a corrective that would prevent civil suits from unjustly damaging reputations.

Cardinal Bernardin's greatest contribution to his church and the

American public may finally be the way in which he handles his ordeal. Already he has responded in a pastoral manner to his accuser, acknowledging what he labels as a clear falsehood against him without condemning Cook. The manner in which Bernardin deals with his suffering will serve as a testimony to the power of faith to sustain the believer.

Presuming his innocence—as people who know him are quick to do—Bernardin must now suffer the public and private anguish of being accused of an act he did not commit. What should sustain him in the months and perhaps years ahead is the realization that it is a central belief in his tradition that unwarranted suffering has its purpose.

Postscript: Subsequent to the initial publication of this essay, Steven Cook recanted his allegations against Cardinal Bernardin. The two men later met, and the cardinal reported that he had forgiven Cook for falsely accusing him. Cook has since died of complications from AIDS. In November 1996, Cardinal Bernardin died of cancer.

GOODNESS AND GREED

The call came in early: the woman on the phone wanted one of the editors to know that she had found his wallet on the street corner. We had all been concerned about the loss, so a message about the good deed went up on the bulletin board. It ended with the observation that "there is still goodness in the land." The woman, whose first name was Mildred, wanted us to know that everything was still in the wallet, including $10 in cash, credit cards and that all-important driver's license. She said she had come into the city to "pay a few bills" when she spotted the wallet. "I didn't want to give it to a policeman," she said, with Chicago-style realism, "so I just waited until this morning to call."

Her act of honesty provides a keynote with which to consider President-elect Bill Clinton's upcoming economic conference in Little Rock. Mildred won't be there, but coordinator Mickey Kantor promises that among the more than 100 participants will be "people who roll up their sleeves, go to work every day and try to make something happen." The nation's big-money people will also be in Little Rock to mingle with the kind of folks who, when they find someone else's wallet on the street, assume that it isn't theirs to keep. The big-money people and the people "who go to work every day" will advise Clinton on ways to address our economic plight.

They should begin their high-powered process by remembering that "there is still goodness in the land." I don't know the names of the people with "rolled-up sleeves" who are being invited to Little Rock, but among them should be some who assume that honesty is better than stealing, and that goodness yields a higher premium than greed. It is, as Ross Perot might say, as simple as that.

And let us assume that among the big-money players at the conference will be those who regard excessive executive salaries and the gambling mentality behind leveraged buyouts as some of the evils that have produced our economic freefall. People, for example, who know firsthand the situation Michael M. Thomas describes: "Capital [is] now concentrated in relatively few hands, so that tens of billions of dollars could be electronically marshaled in a few days to finance all sorts of commission-paying mischief." Thomas makes this observation in the *New York Review of Books* in regard to two books about the leveraged buyout of RJR Nabisco, the nation's 19th-largest corporation. That transaction, says Thomas, "can be seen as the logical, revolting culmination of a process that began some fifteen years earlier."

I was drawn to one of the books Thomas analyzes, *Barbarians at the Gate: The Fall of RJR Nabisco* (HarperCollins, 1990), when I discovered that Vernon Jordan, the chairman of Clinton's transition team, was a member of the board of directors of RJR Nabisco during what has been described as "a classic example of 1980s corporate greed." The book, written by Bryan Burrough and John Helyar, doesn't indict Jordan in any way, other than to note that he was present during that lavish buyout.

Jordan, who began his career as a civil rights leader, has become an important figure in American financial circles through his membership on the RJR Nabisco board and ten other boards. Felix Rohatyn, who has been mentioned for a possible position in the Clinton administration, was the leader of the investment team that helped to conclude the complex $25 billion RJR Nabisco sale, which was financed largely by loans the interest on which was tax-deductible (and thus "covered" by American taxpayers).

Neither Jordan nor Rohatyn is considered a villain in the RJR Nabisco buyout struggle, but they know the game, and they were present at the conclusion of this "commission-paying mischief." One hopes that they will bring their knowledge of corporate mischief to the conference table.

Whenever I wander into fields like this one, which are so complex that every planning meeting must include at least 40 attorneys, I am reminded of the apocryphal story about the young naval officer in World War II who was sitting in while the admirals were discussing ways to protect Allied shipping from elusive German submarines. The young officer raised his hand, was recognized, and then said he had the solution: "Heat the Atlantic Ocean to the boiling point and the submarines would all have to surface, whereupon we will destroy them all." Stunned by this, one admiral finally blurted out, "Just how do you propose to heat the water?" To which the young officer replied, "I have told you how to solve the problem; you will have to work out the details."

Experienced leaders like Jordan and Rohatyn, along with Clinton's economic transition leader Robert Reich, will have to work out the details. They will have to propose ways for Congress to curb the excesses of American corporations, including the sort that led to the RJR Nabisco buyout which left defeated CEO Ross Johnson with a severance package of somewhere between $30 million and $60 million. Johnson had ingratiated himself with his board members and executives by offering the use of corporate jets on occasions when commercial coach would have served the purpose.

The economic conference will need to find ways to reduce the temptations to pursue greed in American business. Fairness, not profit alone, should be a factor in making sure that medical costs are controlled and that insurance companies are not permitted to arbitrarily cut off protection for catastrophic illnesses.

The RJR Nabisco buyout has become a symbol of American corporate greed, in which a few receive enormous profits without regard for the well-being of the community. Greed of this magnitude need not be the model for American business in finding solutions to our economic doldrums. Goodness is better than greed, and it is possible to live with goodness as a personal and corporate guide. If we could just combine Mildred's honesty with the entrepreneurial skills of American business, we might find our economy recovering faster than we expect.

A TIME TO BE BORN

A 59-year-old woman told a California infertility clinic that she was only 50, and four years later gave birth to a baby girl. The clinic, which sets 55 as the maximum age for patients seeking a donated egg, was fooled by the woman's relatively young appearance and her falsified documents. At the time of the birth, she was 63. This was her first child. She had given up her job at a bank in order to become a mother. Her husband, 57, provided the sperm for the conception. The clinic charged $50,000 for its services.

Reactions to the oldest woman to give birth are varied. Dr. Willard Gaylin of the Hastings Center, which specializes in medical ethics, told the *New York Times* he finds pregnancies in women who are past menopause distasteful. "I certainly understand a desire for progeny," he said, " but I do feel we have a responsibility to the symmetry of life and to some of the rules of nature." Dr. David M. Buss, a psychology professor at the University of Texas at Austin, took an informal poll among friends and discovered that women reacted to this late-in-life parenting with a hearty "Go for it," while the men he queried "furrowed their brows and said it was repugnant."

Anthropologist Barbara Koenig of Stanford University told the *Times* that "technology is challenging some fundamental assumptions" about the sexuality of older women. Gilbert C. Meilaender, a theologian at Valparaiso University, hesitated to say that it is wrong to bear a child at that age, but feels that "it just doesn't seem fitting." To Meilaender, the pregnancy "captures our sense that there is a kind of unwillingness or inability to come to terms with what the trajectory of a life really is."

A few days after the story about the 63-year-old mother appeared, 77-year-old actor Tony Randall posed proudly with his new daughter, thereby raising the obvious question: If men can do it, and be proud of it, why can't women? *Newsweek* quoted writer Katha Pollitt: "Until we are ready to severely castigate the so-called start-over dads, I think we can't be too judgmental and moralistic about women who avail themselves of technology that exists." One quick answer to this, of course, is that older men don't need to make use of medical technology to father a child. And the man's partner is presumably premenopausal, which means that one parent is likely to be healthy and energetic enough to raise the child.

A theme running through much of this discussion is the sanctity of individual desires. What matters from an individualistic perspective is personal fulfillment, the joy of bringing new life into the world, and the production of progeny. This is the mind-set that says: If science can give it to me, I will take it. Buss of the University of Texas puts it this way: "I believe people should live their lives whatever way they want to." So pervasive is this individualistic thrust in our culture that the burden of proof rests on those who would set limits on the fulfillment of human desires.

Christians don't have particular biblical texts that deal with the birthing process, though we do have the reminder from Ecclesiastes that "for everything there is a season, and a time for every matter under heaven: a time to be born, and a time to die." When the natural seasons and processes of life are interrupted in the Bible—when Sarah gives birth to Isaac in her old age, when an angel tells Mary she will have a child—the intent is to identify a miracle from God, not to argue ethics.

Can older parents offer a reasonable promise of providing care for two decades? Is it fair to the child to have parents who are statistically likely to be dead by the time the child reaches puberty? Of course, a child born to a responsible mother in her 60s will get a better start in life than the child of an 18-year-old crack cocaine addict. Many youngsters can testify that when they were abandoned by teenage mothers, their grandmothers gave them a stable home life. Still, what is the impact of postmenopausal births on the larger community? Doesn't the happiness of the individual parent need to be weighed against the good of the community?

We might also consider Immanuel Kant's moral imperative: that we should act only on principles that we can will to be universal principles. (Or, as your mother once said, in her updating of Kantian philosophy: "Don't throw that candy wrapper on the sidewalk; what if everybody did that?") In this case, we should consider what society would be like if everybody said: If science can provide it, I will take it.

The argument against using reproductive technology beyond reasonable limits turns finally on the definition of reasonable. And who determines and enforces what is reasonable? Governmental agencies already establish some age limits to govern personal behavior. There are, for example, age requirements about voting, buying alcohol and cigarettes, getting a driver's license, and getting married. But our society has been reluctant to set limits for the practice of medicine, preferring to have the profession set its own standards.

As an alternative to enacting legal controls over reproductive technology, a national commission of scientists, doctors and citizens is needed, a commission that could develop voluntary ethical guidelines. Guidelines could be written that would respect the individual rights of citizens eager to benefit from current and future medical and technological advances, but would also put individual rights in the context of the well-being of the larger community. We have considerable national resources with which to develop these guidelines, including our tradition of justice and fair play, our respect for individual rights and the common good, and—not least—the wisdom of the eloquent writer who left us those eloquent words about the natural rhythms of life: "For everything there is a season."

HOPES AND FEARS

"The hopes and fears of all the years are met in thee tonight."

Phillips Brooks

EXPECTANT WAITING

A radio correspondent was droning on about the economic problems facing an African nation. She concluded her summary with the phrase, "We'll just have to wait and see what happens." I suddenly realized I had been hearing that cliché in a great variety of situations lately. It has become as irritating as "Have a nice day."

When the doctor says the cancer has grown to the point that medication is no longer effective, the phrase is hauled out: we'll just have to wait and see what happens. As a concluding comment to a report or a conversation, the admonition implies passivity. When we wait to see what happens in this African state or that baseball trade or this medical condition, we are letting unknown forces assume command and deliver a final result. The matter is no longer in our hands.

Terry Anderson is a living testimony that waiting need not mean passivity. For six years he was forced to wait in a dark cell, sometimes alone, often chained. His captors were brutal. They tortured him, physically and mentally. How did he respond? "You just do what you have to do," he said to reporters when he arrived in Damascus. "You wake up every day, summon up the energy from somewhere and you get through the day, day after day after day."

There were periods when he said he felt like giving up, overwhelmed with despair at the suffering and hopelessness of his condition. But he was not passive. His was a waiting of active expectancy, even though there was no clear vision of how or when the story would end. He filled his horribly truncated existence in dogged pursuit of growth. From fellow prisoner Thomas Sutherland he learned to speak French. From his captors he learned more Arabic. When guards took away slips of paper he had fashioned into playing cards, he created a makeshift chess set. An avid weightlifter before his capture, Anderson used two plastic water bottles to simulate dumbbells.

The first book he was allowed to have was a Bible, which he devoured. In dialogue with fellow captives he regained the Catholic faith of his youth. When asked what kept him going, he points to the people who were with him, his faith and his stubbornness. Brian Keenan, an Irishman held with Anderson until August 1990, offers some insight into the kind of waiting he experienced with his fellow hostage.

Keenan described Anderson as "a bit of a bulky and belligerent newspaper man who had a voracious hunger for intellectual conversation, and when he did not get it, he would pace the floor endlessly in his patched, repatched and even more patched but still very holely socks." When the inevitable periods of despair descended, Keenan and Anderson would spend hours talking of Anderson's daughter, born a few months after he was seized in Beirut in 1985.

There was nothing Anderson could do to escape or break the physical bonds that held him, but he retained control of how he viewed those bonds. When he writes his promised book on his ordeal, we will learn more of what he thought and felt through the years of captivity. Meanwhile, he testifies that we never just have to wait and see; as long as we can hope we are not trapped into passive waiting.

This is the season when we wait expectantly for the mystery of Christmas, when we wait to celebrate the coming of the Christ child whose gift of himself has forever removed the hopelessness of passive waiting. The Christmas mystery is not confined to a single day or season, though we need those calendar days to prompt us to recall that there is never a moment when nothing more can be done. There is always Advent, the active waiting for the light of full union with God—a God whose presence at Bethlehem is our guarantee that no human bondage can ever lock us into just waiting for whatever comes next.

Terry Anderson has given us a gift this Christmas. In his years of confinement he was building more than chess sets and patching more than holely socks. He was providing a model for expectant waiting.

NOT AFRAID TO FAIL

Rarely has the signing of a minor league baseball prospect—especially one who is 31 years old and hasn't played baseball since high school—provoked such a stir. But this, of course, was no ordinary prospect. It was Michael Jordan, the world's greatest basketball player, who will try out for the Chicago White Sox at spring training. What happens if he fails? a reporter asked. "I am not afraid to fail," Michael said. With that response, Jordan accepted an even greater challenge than leading the Chicago Bulls to three straight National Basketball Association championships. "I am not afraid to fail" may not enjoy the permanence of Grantland Rice's "It matters not whether you win or lose, but how you play the game," but it is a refreshing addition to the lexicon of a usually cynical sports world.

What makes Jordan's plunge into baseball significant is that almost everyone except Jordan expects him to fail. The Chicago White Sox management must know this. Anyone even remotely cognizant of what it takes to hit major league pitching, or even minor league pitching, knows his chances of playing professional baseball are remote. Still, he is going to risk his worldwide reputation. He is not afraid to fail.

Jordan is getting his chance not because he has demonstrated superior baseball skills but because he is Michael Jordan. He has no baseball experience, and has given no indication that he can hit, field, bunt, or steal bases. But because he is Michael Jordan he has earned the right to try—and the right to fail.

Stow away Michael's phrase for this year's graduation speeches. Use it when your daughter says she is not good enough to try out for her school's basketball team. Reflect upon it when you are offered a job that demands skills you think you don't have. Jordan offers living testimony that successful people are ones who look for a challenge.

Personal challenges can be as close as the next step we take. For most of us walking is automatic, but not so for the woman whose leg has been amputated. The failures we are willing to risk vary according to circumstance. Which pain, or sorrow, or disappointment do we need to face? It is easy to avoid facing our own particular fear of not making it.

What is our greatest fear? Whether we realize it or not, we are all afraid of one thing: not being authentic to ourselves. The effort to live up to self-designed expectations is at the heart of personal wholeness. To speak of authenticity in this manner is not to raise the question of a proper vocation or the achievement of excellence. It refers, rather, to the need for congruity between inner self and outward behavior. As we grow older, it is easier to live according to minimum expectations, rather than rise to the challenge of matching inner dreams with outward behavior. Authenticity equals possibility; inauthenticity leads us to deadness.

While doing research for his book *The Spiritual Life of Children*, Robert Coles talked with children too young to have become encrusted by an adult's aloofness from feelings. He found children still willing to explore "the eternal whys of this life." One young girl told Coles:

> I saw our neighbor, and he'd been in an accident, and he told my dad that he'd just as soon die now as later, because of all the pain he has. His stomach hurts all the time. He's got the worst back pain you can imagine. I wondered what it would be like to have all that pain—to be hurting by day and by night . . . The funny thing—our neighbor, he smiles, despite his troubles. He's glad he can see the sun come up in the morning, my mom says. Today I saw the sun coming up, and I was glad, and I thought, I should be double glad, because I can see it, and I love the way the whole sky becomes lit up, presto, and I don't have any pain . . .
>
> I saw a tree fall last week. Some serious wind came blowing, and crack, it went: sounded like someone shooting his rifle off yonder! When a tree goes—that's life too . . . My mother says I asked her when I was real little if a tree hurts, or a rock. She said no, they don't. She said I came back at her with: "Mommy, God must hurt when a tree is in trouble."

I remembered that interview when I heard Jordan tell the media he was not afraid of failure. I also remembered my own sense of failure when a large tree in our yard lost a major limb during a storm. It seemed to me I could have saved that noble old limb on which children had climbed and which had been the source of shade for so many years. I could have had the tree trimmed, reducing its vulnerability to wind and rain. I grieved for that limb because its loss represented a personal failure, a deed not done. Perhaps my action could have made the difference.

What connects my crippled tree to a risk-taking Michael Jordan? I find the answer in the simple formula: try, even if you make a mistake. Don't turn away from a challenge. Not to act could produce a result more painful than failure.

At some point in the next few months, Michael Jordan's venture into professional baseball will reach a crossroad. He will either succeed or face the fact of failure. I can't write Michael's theology for him, but I can identify with him as he faces the possibility of failure—the possibility that the world's greatest basketball player will be cut from a minor league baseball team. When he says he is not afraid to fail, I believe he is telling the truth. That's why this gifted athlete deserves to be mentioned in graduation speeches: his real fear is not of failure, but of not trying.

STILL NOT AFRAID TO FAIL

Reporters in Chicago have treated Michael Jordan's return to basketball as a story of biblical proportions. Some columnists have been so bold as to suggest that Jordan is a new Moses, called to lead the Bulls out of the wilderness. Others have hinted that given the state of professional sports, Jordan is a messiah, come to redeem the fallen.

There are some other biblical categories we might apply to Jordan Redux. Two parables especially come to mind. The first is, as biblical scholars are wont to say, the more problematic: we might see

Michael Jordan as the prodigal son who has returned home to a joyous reception, surrounded by tumultuous fans who pour out their adoration and forgive him for forsaking basketball for the far-off country of professional baseball.

The analogy doesn't really fit, though, since Jordan did not squander his inheritance in "loose living." (But if you are a Bulls fan who watched the Jordanless Bulls fail to win the 1994 championship and then hover around .500 this season, Jordan's investment in baseball was big-time squandering.) And Jordan's teammates, who might be expected to play the role of the elder brother and be disgruntled now that they will get less playing time, seem excited to have him back. Winning a championship without Jordan was a slim prospect at best; now there is a chance.

A more relevant parable is the one about the talents. Jesus describes a "man going on a journey [who] called his servants and entrusted to them his property," and gave them money, "each according to his ability." The workers blessed with five and two talents used them to make more money and promptly doubled their original gift. When the master returned they were duly praised. Meanwhile, the worker entrusted with only one talent, seized with an overwhelming fear of failure and knowing that his master was a "hard man," decided not to risk any loss. He dug a hole and put his talent in the ground. At this the master was furious. By not trying, the frightened worker had not made progress with the limited resources he possessed.

Jordan is not one to bury his talent. He makes the most of what he has. And as he told us upon embarking on his baseball career, he is "not afraid to fail."

There is a scene in the film *Chariots of Fire* in which Harold Abrahams, the British track star, loses a 100-meter heat. For a long time afterwards he sits in the empty stands staring at the track. He recalls the pain of the moment when an opponent crossed the finish line a fraction of a second in front of him. Sybil Gordon, his future wife, offers consolation, but Abrahams turns to her and says, "If I can't win, I won't run." Sybil retorts, "If you don't run, you can't win." Stung back to reality, Abrahams goes on to win the finals and eventually becomes the only Englishman ever to win an Olympic sprint title.

On every NBA team there are players with talent. Though few can approach Jordan's natural skills, the degree of their success has more to do with what they do with their talents than how much talent they have been given. Even at the NBA level, players fail to reach their potential. A fear of failure often makes players adopt a cautious, tentative stance.

When Jordan left basketball he was the league's pre-eminent star; in baseball, his talents were untested. The danger of failure loomed large, but he told skeptics he was not afraid to fail. Now that Jordan has returned to basketball, he is once again in danger of failure. He may not live up to expectations: his skills may be diminished; he may not have the stamina to match younger players; capturing a fourth NBA title, which many expect the Bulls to do, may be beyond his grasp.

Jordan's willingness to risk failure again has not gone unnoticed among some of the young basketball fans who live in the African-American neighborhood around the Bulls' stadium on Chicago's West Side. Tyrone Collier, an 11-year-old junior high school student who attends an after-school program, was asked by the *Chicago Tribune* what he thought of Jordan's return. Collier replied, "He never thinks, 'What if I go in and mess up? He thinks, 'I'm going to do better for my team and myself.'" Steve House, 15, commented: "There's a lot of people who say, 'You can't do this because you're too short' or 'Your feet are too big.' But if you try your best, you can accomplish anything. . . . In baseball, Jordan tried his best. It didn't quite work out for him the way he wanted. He didn't fail to me."

Michael Turnipseed, 15, said he is inspired by Jordan both for his basketball playing and his willingness to try. He has learned from Jordan that "if I try, I can't fail." When Jordan and the Bulls lost to the Orlando Magic in Jordan's third game after his return, Turnipseed took the loss philosophically: "They'll be ready for the next game tomorrow." (They were: in that game Jordan's last-second shot gave Chicago a one-point victory.)

Charles Barkley, who plays for the Phoenix Suns, insists that professional sports stars should not be expected to be role models for young people. But this is not a choice Barkley can make. Highly visible sports figures will inevitably be role models. Students from Chicago's West Side look to Michael Jordan as more than a model for playing basketball. They see in him two talents they need both on and off the court: a positive attitude in confronting adversity, and a determination to keep trying.

The return of this particular prodigal son allows us to note once again that Michael Jordan is not afraid to fail. Jordan reminds us that the higher we go the greater the danger of falling—but he also reminds us that, at any level, not trying is worse than the greatest failure.

STORIES THAT SHAPE US

To atone for the sin of missing all of my previous high school class reunions, I was asked to give a talk at the most recent gathering. I returned to Monroe, Georgia, and met up with those who had been thrown together with me for those four intense years in which children move into being adults. As anyone who has ever attended such an event knows, it's a jarring experience to walk into a room and confront adults you haven't seen since they were teenagers. What's striking is not just how much they (and you) have changed in appearance, but how the years do fall away and faded memories are revived and restored. What psychologists term "dated emotions" are no longer dated; they are current and real.

I spoke to my classmates about the different stories we live by—the "narratives," as scholars term them these days, that shape us. Henry Louis Gates Jr. says that "people arrive at an understanding of themselves and the world through narratives—narratives purveyed by schoolteachers, newscasters, 'authorities,' and all the other authors of our common sense."

A dramatic change in the narratives we live by has been documented by Alan Ehrenhalt in his book *The Lost City* (see earlier reference, p. 99). Comparing attitudes of today to those of the 1950s, he found that people of the '90s expect to have a wider array of choices; are less committed to the choices they do make; are more suspicious of authority; and don't take the idea of personal sin as seriously.

Earlier generations did not always make good choices, Ehrenhalt notes. Its commitments were at times as shaky as those made today; authority was resented for its heavy-handedness; and a strong notion of sin did not prevent people from sinning. Nevertheless, the narratives that shaped those earlier generations took commitment, authority and sin seriously. People responded with genuine feelings of guilt and shame when they violated the edicts of their communities.

Before I went to the reunion, I saw *Strange Days*, a film which portrays a chilling future in which a new extreme in entertainment escapism has been attained through a technology that taps into a person's emotional center and captures immediate experiences that are retained on a film clip. This experience of virtual reality is then preserved for future viewing. Mace, played by Angela Bassett, resists the new technology and tells her boyfriend, Lenny, "Memories are meant to fade, they're designed that way for a reason."

Mace is only partly correct. I discovered at the reunion that memories do fade, but given the proper stimulation they can become vivid again. We don't need artificial preservation on videotape to recall earlier memories. And what we once saw darkly may become a far more enriching experience because of the added dimension mature experience offers.

For example, I remember that during fourth grade I was seriously ill with typhoid fever. (I still have trouble with Roman numerals because they were covered during my extended absence, and none of my other teachers ever returned to that topic.) One high school student died from typhoid in the Monroe epidemic, and death haunted the town. What I hadn't realized until the recent class reunion was the degree to which the children who did not get typhoid lived in constant fear that they, too, would get sick and die.

One of my classmates remembered that since she lived near my house, she was assigned the task of bringing homework to me each day I was out of school. She remembered how my mother would have to "wash" all of my books to "kill the germs." She also recalled that she sat next to me in class on the day I got sick, and how she feared she would be the next victim. Despite her fears, she dutifully served as my homework courier. (My classmate is a nurse now and knows that the typhoid germ was in the unpasteurized milk we drank, not on the books we touched.) No doubt children today are capable of accepting serious assignments despite their fears, but the narratives that prevail today do not put a premium on such conduct.

Thirty-five out of 49 living graduates attended the reunion. We didn't have time to delve deeply into our personal lives, but I am prepared to assume that most of us have tried to pass along our narratives—including what shaped us as high school students—to our children and grandchildren. I am also convinced, however, that the culture has not encouraged us to stress the importance of commitment and authority or the reality and consequences of sin.

Our generation was no different from any others; we made our mistakes and far too often ignored the wisdom that acts have consequences. We did have, however, a strong sense of the seriousness of sin.

I remember one incident that suggested how much sin and authority mattered then as compared to now: I was shooting pool at the pool hall one day. Whenever I frequented the place I did so with a general feeling of unease. On this particular day I looked up to see the Methodist minister walk into the room. I have no idea what brought him there. I do know that I panicked and pushed my cue stick into someone else's hand and stepped quickly away from the table. Unfortunately, the boy I handed the stick to was wearing a jacket, gloves and a cap; he was getting ready to step outside. Clearly, he was not the shooter. In that moment I was guilty of two sins: the minor one of shooting pool, and the more important sin of deceit. Sin and authority came together in that moment and became a permanent part of my personal narrative.

It would be misleading to suggest that my class lived a superior moral existence because it took sin seriously. The fact that our reunion included no African-Americans illustrates that we were part of a segregated school system. We were, however, also members of a generation that lived through the period in which segregation was ended by a few courageous acts of defiance and finally by law—a change related to, and supported by, the same sense of sin, grounded in the biblical narrative that shaped our childhoods.

Though we cannot return to the virtual reality of our high school years, we can also never leave that reality behind. We are who we are because of the people and the narratives that shaped us. The memories won't fade, because they are of moments that made us who we are.

FAMILY CONNECTIONS

A ten-year-old boy stood quietly next to his mother's grave in a family cemetery at the top of a mountain overlooking the Savannah River. Just six weeks earlier the boy had been to the cemetery for another burial service—for his grandfather. The boy's name was McKendree Tucker. It's possible, of course, that the boy didn't attend both funerals; there's no written record on this. But I do know that his mother and grandfather are buried close together in the family plot in Elbert County, Georgia, a few miles from the South Carolina border, and that McKendree was ten when his mother died.

Church records indicate that the boy's father, Eppes Tucker, served as a minister in the early 1800s on Methodist circuits in South Carolina and Georgia. McKendree was most likely named for his father's presiding elder, William McKendree, who years later became the first native-born American bishop in the Methodist Episcopal Church. I like to ponder the facts about McKendree Tucker, because he is my grandfather's grandfather.

Family reunions are a time to contemplate the past, and some members of my mother's family did that recently. We met, as we have been doing occasionally over the past few decades, in Georgia, this time at St. Simons Island. This is where John and Charles Wesley came in 1735. They were sent, one source puts it, "to oversee the spiritual lives of the colonists and to missionize the Indians as an agent for the Society for the Propagation of the Gospel." The two Anglican priests had been invited to Georgia by Colonel James Oglethorpe, governor of the colony.

Garrison Keillor was also in Georgia the weekend of our family reunion. One of the stories he told was about John Wesley's unsuccessful romantic pursuit of 18-year-old Sophia Hopkey, one of Wesley's more devout parishioners and the niece of the chief magistrate of Savannah. Wesley couldn't make up his mind whether clergy should marry, so Sophia lost interest. She began to miss services and communion ("nine times in two months"). When she did return to worship, Wesley, "fully aware of the consequences," refused to serve her communion. This strict adherence to rules was typical of Wesley, who was quite "methodical" in his religious practice.

Wesley did not remain long in Georgia. Whether because of romantic disappointment or other reasons, he and Charles went back to England in 1737, never to return to the colonies except through the enthusiasm of their Methodist followers who soon powerfully influenced the religious life of the new nation.

As one of two Methodist preachers attending our family reunion, I was asked to provide a homily at the closing family worship service. I decided to speak about family and the church, and about family stories. Family connections are fragile, and they can easily slip away unless attention is paid. What better time to solidify these connections than at a family reunion?

I suggested that we imagine ourselves with McKendree Tucker next to his mother's grave on that summer day in 1818. (I should note that I came up with this brainstorming technique without the aid of New Age counselors, and that it is perfectly normal to seek an imaginative, revitalizing link to the past.) McKendree's father continued to "itinerate," as the Methodists describe the practice of traveling preachers, in South Carolina until the three generations of Tuckers moved to Alabama's Chambers County. McKendree and his wife, Elizabeth, had seven sons and three daughters. Their oldest daughter was Martha Elizabeth, my grandfather's mother.

I also told family members that along with a devout spirit, McKendree Tucker had left us with a genetic tendency to rebel. He withdrew from the Methodist Episcopal Church to help start the Methodist Protestant Church, an offshoot formed in protest against the Methodist Episcopal Church's refusal to allow the laity to participate in district and conference voting for the selection of bishops. During the Civil War McKendree dispensed community funds to widows, orphans and others in need. After the war, his property destroyed, grieving over two sons killed in battle, one at Murfreesboro, Tennessee, and the other at Chancellorsville, McKendree took an oath of allegiance to again become a citizen of the United States.

A few years ago I went to the courthouse in Chambers County,

Alabama, and looked at the document signed by my grandfather's grandfather in 1865: "I, McKendree Tucker, do solemnly swear that I will henceforth faithfully support, protect and defend the Constitution of the United States and the Union of States thereunder; and that I will, in like manner, abide by and support all laws and proclamations which have been made during the existing rebellion with reference to the emancipation of slaves. So help me God."

About a year before McKendree's death, according to a family history written by his brother Coke, McKendree's "love for Mount Jefferson and his passion for preaching broke over physical barriers . . . and he said he must preach at Mount Jefferson [Church] once more. He told the congregation he would preach on 'Heaven,' that ever-lasting good home of the righteous." Coke Tucker quotes from that sermon, and though the words may reflect Coke's memories more than the actual speech, I suggested that we let that sermon be our final word:

> Heaven . . . will be my theme til this poor soul and stammering tongue lies silent, silent in death. Heaven, the home of the good, like myself you will have one or more friends there. Oh, the solid solace the thought imparts to any poor soul, that someday, not far distant, my soul, severed from this poor old worn-out body, shall soar away to Heaven of eternal rest for which I have labored for more than 60 years. I know this is the last time I shall ever address you. So dear friends, Good night. When most of us meet again, it will be good morning, thank God.

I don't know how those words sounded to the younger members of our family, but the oldest member of the family who came to worship at St. Simons put it this way: "Now I feel connected." So did I. I felt connected to McKendree, to the mother he lost at age ten, to his two sons who died in battle, to my grandfather, to John and Charles Wesley, and even to Sophia Hopkey. Just imagine, had Sophia married John Wesley in 1735, he might have settled down as a contented Anglican priest in the New World. And without the Methodists, would there have been the great revivals of the early 19th century? Who would have started all those colleges along the frontier? Connections made, and connections not made, are mysterious to ponder. Especially at family reunions.